STUDENT SOFTWARE WORKSHEET MANUAL

ELBERT B. GREYNOLDS
Southern Methodist University

EIGHTH EDITION

STRATEGIC MARKETING PROBLEMS

CASES AND COMMENTS

ROGER A. KERIN

ROBERT A. PETERSON

PRENTICE HALL, UPPER SADDLE RIVER, NJ 07458

Acquisitions editor: Whitney Blake
Associate editor: John Larkin
Project editor: Richard Bretan
Manufacturing buyer: Ken Clinton

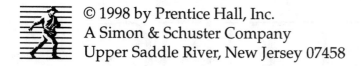 © 1998 by Prentice Hall, Inc.
A Simon & Schuster Company
Upper Saddle River, New Jersey 07458

Printed in the United States of America

10 9 8 7 6 5 4 3 2 1

ISBN 0-13-678772-X

Prentice-Hall International (UK) Limited, *London*
Prentice-Hall of Australia Pty. Limited, *Sydney*
Prentice-Hall Canada Inc., *Toronto*
Prentice-Hall Hispanoamericana, S.A., *Mexico*
Prentice-Hall of India Private Limited, *New Delhi*
Prentice-Hall of Japan, Inc., *Tokyo*
Simon & Schuster Asia Pte. Ltd., *Singapore*
Editora Prentice-Hall do Brasil, Ltda., *Rio de Janeiro*

Table of Contents

CONTENTS

Computer Assisted Applications and Worksheets

Part I -- How to Use Manual and Worksheets

Chapter 1: Introduction 1
Chapter 2: Sample Case - Hasty Tasty 3
    Introduction..3
SAMPLE CASE - HASTY TASTY 3
Introduction to How Worksheets are Setup 5
How to Use the Worksheet 5
Viewing The Spreadsheet Calculations 7
Saving the Spreadsheet 7
Printing The Worksheet 7
Input Form for Sample Case - Hasty Tasty 8
Output Form for Sample Case - Hasty Tasty...9
CHAPTER 3: Introduction to Spreadsheets 10
Introduction...10
Computer Lab Procedures 10
Location of Disk Drives..11
Floppy disks..11
How to Turn on a Computer That has a Hard Disk 12
Start Windows Program...13
Microsoft Specific Instructions..13
    How to Start Microsoft Excel in Windows 3.1 14
    How to Start Microsoft Excel in Windows 95 14
    Accessing Menus with Keystrokes 15
    Open Worksheet File Menu 16
    Set Disk Drive and Load Worksheet..16
    How to Save the Microsoft Excel Spreadsheet..19
    How to Exit Microsoft Excel 19
    Set Navigation Keys Option 19
Lotus 1-2-3 Specific Instructions..19
    How to Start Lotus 1-2-3 in Windows...19
    Accessing Menus with Keystrokes 20
    Open Worksheet File Menu 21
    Set Disk Drive and Load Worksheet..22
    How to Save the Lotus 1-2-3 Spreadsheet 23
    How to Exit Lotus 1-2-3 24
Spreadsheet Techniques Common to Lotus 1-2-3 and Microsoft Excel 24
    Using the Keyboard Keys with a Spreadsheet...24
    Spreadsheet Data Entry 26
    Simple Equations 26
    Function Keys 27
    Keystroke Tables 27
    Clear Worksheet Screen...28

Table of Contents

SAMPLE.WK1 Worksheet Example 28
How to Enter Data Into the Worksheet...29
Type Values in Spreadsheet From Input Form 30
Examine Reports...31
Save the Worksheet Results..32
Macros in Case Worksheets...33
How to Print a Worksheet With Macro Command..33
How to Split the Windows in the Worksheet...33
Graphs 35
How to Change the Column Width on a Worksheet 37
Using Goal Seek for What-If Analysis 38
Goal Seek Analysis in Excel...38
Goal Seek Analysis in Lotus 1-2-3 40

Part II -- Worksheets for General Case Analysis

Chapter 4: Break Even Analysis -- One Product 43
Chapter 5: Break Even Analysis -- Two Products 48
Chapter 6: Break Even Analysis -- Three Products 54
Chapter 7: 60
Cannibalization Assessment 60
Chapter 8: Sales Forecast -- Units 64
Chapter 9: Sales Forecast - Dollars...69
Chapter 10: Regression Analysis 74

Part III -- Worksheets for Cases

CHAPTER 11: Pharmacia & Upjohn, Inc.: Rogaine Hair Regrowth Treatment 80
Chapter 12: South Delaware Coors, Inc..85
Chapter 13: Soft and Silky Shaving Gel 91
Chapter 14: Frito-Lay's Dips..96
Chapter 15: Perpetual Care Hospital: Downtown Health Clinic 101
Chapter 16: Swisher Mower and Machine Company 106
Chapter 17: Carrington Furniture, Inc. (B) 111
Chapter 18: Cadbury Beverages, Inc.: CRUSH Brand 115
Chapter 19: Southwest Airlines 119
Chapter 20: Atlas Electronics Corporation 127
Chapter 21: Augustine Medical, Inc.: Bair Hugger 131
Chapter 22: North Pittsburgh Telephone Company..138
Chapter 23: The Circle K Corporation...143
Chapter 24: Macon Institutue of Art and History 147
Chapter 25: Show Circuit Frozen Dog Dinner 153
Chapter 26: Cima Mountaineering..162
Chapter 27: Colgate-Palmolive Canada: Arctic Power Detergent.......................167

Chapter 1:
Introduction

Computer spreadsheet or worksheet software programs can significantly aid and improve the quality of marketing analysis and decision making. Students graduating with business degrees should be proficient with computer spreadsheet analysis using popular programs such as Microsoft Excel, or Lotus 1-2-3. This manual and its worksheets demonstrates to students how a spreadsheet program such as Microsoft Excel or Lotus 1-2-3 can aid decision making by marketing managers. It also develops the student's skill in working with spreadsheets.

This manual contains all the material necessary to use Microsoft Excel or Lotus 1-2-3 for case analysis, except of course the spreadsheet programs themselves. The manual is divided into three parts.

Part I - How to Use the Manual and Worksheets

> Chapters 1, 2, and 3 make up Part I. Chapter 2 contains a sample case, Hasty Tasty, which is used to demonstrate how to use the spreadsheets in this manual for case analysis.
>
> Chapter 3 contains instructions on operating a computer and Lotus 1-2-3, or Microsoft Excel spreadsheet programs for use with the worksheets provided in this manual. In this chapter you learn how to:

> - Turn on the computer and load the spreadsheet program.
> - Use basic spreadsheet commands.
> - Use the worksheets provided in this manual for case analysis.
> - Save the worksheets.
> - Print the results of your analysis.
> - What-If analysis

Part II - Worksheets for General Case Analysis

> Chapters 4 through 10 make up Part II and contain Lotus 1-2-3 worksheets that you can use with Microsoft Excel and instructions for general case analysis in four areas: break even analysis and contribution margin analysis, cannibalization assessment, sales forecasting, and linear regression analysis.

Part III - Worksheets for Cases

> Chapters 11 through 27 make up Part III and contain worksheets and instructions for specific cases included in the case book, **Strategic Marketing Problems: Cases and Comments, 8th. ed.** written by Roger Kerin and Robert Peterson. Professor Kerin has assisted me in developing the worksheets contained in this manual. His effort and advice is greatly appreciated.

Each worksheet in the manual has input forms and output forms for recording analysis results.

A graph is included as part of many worksheets in this manual. However, you must use a computer that can display graphics for this feature to be seen on your display screen.

The Microsoft Excel spreadsheet program file format is used in this manual because it has become an industry standard. Also included are duplicate files in the Lotus 1-2-3 for Windows WK4 format. Hence, either Microsoft Excel or Lotus 1-2-3 for Windows is the appropriate program for this manual. Many other spreadsheet programs are either Microsoft Excel or Lotus 1-2-3 compatible and can read the file for this text from disk. The worksheets in this manual, are compatible with Microsoft Excel Version 5.0 and higher, or Lotus versions 4.0 and higher. To use these templates with Quattro Pro make sure you identify the files as either XLS or WK4 formats before loading them.

The macros in the worksheets are linked to buttons you push to print either the worksheet or the graph. Just click on the button to execute the macro.

If you use Microsoft Excel to access the spreadsheets in this book, then make sure you set the Navigation Keys option. This option makes the program use the navigation keys (e.g., Home, End) the same as the Lotus 1-2-3 program. The menu location for version 5 of Excel is:

Excel Version 5.0
Menu Location

- Tools
- Options
- Transition Navigation Keys
- Turn on option

Begin using this manual, by first reading the sample case, Hasty Tasty, and work through the introductory material in Chapter 3. After completing that material, you are ready to use Microsoft Excel or Lotus 1-2-3 with any of the cases included in this manual.

Chapter 2:
Sample Case - Hasty Tasty

Introduction

The Hasty Tasty case demonstrates how to use Microsoft Excel or Lotus 1-2-3 for Windows to enhance your financial analysis of a case. Please read this case carefully. The instructions on how to use the spreadsheets follow this section of the manual.

SAMPLE CASE - HASTY TASTY

by Irvin A. Zaenglein

Northern Michigan University

Nestled on the Southern shoreline of Lake Superior, the town of Munising, Michigan is a major draw for tourists. Hasty Tasty is just one of many businesses in the area which capitalizes on tourism.

Hasty Tasty sells ice cream and fast foods such as pastries, hot dogs, submarine sandwiches, and soft drinks on a take-out basis from the first of May through Labor Day. It provides an outdoor, picnic atmosphere seating area for customers, but does not have indoor accommodations for customers to consume their purchases. Parking is not a problem.

In the same building is a printing business and a small game arcade operation. Each is run separately. The game operation and the Hasty Tasty outlet both face Munising Avenue, the highway which runs through town. The print shop is in the rear of the building.

In September the owners of Hasty Tasty (Gary and Donna Snedeker) were reflecting on the just completed season. It was a good year, but the Snedekers were considering additional ways of reaching their target markets. The two best alternatives appeared to be serving their products from a truck at Sand Point and/or Miner's Castle.

SAND POINT

Located on Lake Superior within Pictured Rocks National Lakeshore, Sand Point is a recreational area open to the general public at no charge and is used primarily as a swimming beach. It is approximately 3.5 miles from Hasty Tasty to Sand Point. Only one road goes to the Sand Point beach.

The Park Service estimates that 38,001 people visited Sand Point during the summer (i.e., June, July, August) of this year. That number is obtained by counting the number of vehicles passing over a counter in the road, subtracting the number of times employees drive over the counter, and dividing by two (i.e., an auto would drive over the counter going to the beach and then again leaving). The Park Service has determined that there are approximately 3.5 people in each auto visiting Sand Point, thus the number of autos is multiplied by a factor of 3.5 to estimate the number of people visiting Sand Point in a given month. The number of visitors to Sand Point during the summer is as follows:

Month	Number of Visitors
June	7,777
July	14,904
August	15,320

Total: 38,001

While some of the visitors are tourists, some are from the nearby community. The Park Service does not have data estimating what percentage of the visitors to Sand Point are tourists. While data about peak hours are not available, the Park Rangers feel that 2-5 PM might be the peak usage hours followed by 11 AM-2 PM, and that the third most heavily used time period might be from 5-8 PM. It felt that usage of the beach is minimal before 11 am and after 8 PM.

MINER'S CASTLE

The Miner's Castle is a rock formation on the Lake Superior shoreline which resembles a castle. It is part of the Pictured Rocks National Park Service, and is open to the public at no charge. Miner's Castle is approximately 11.0 miles from Hasty Tasty. There is only one entrance/exit road to Miner's Castle. The same procedure as for Sand Point is employed in the counting of visitors to the area. The numbers for this summer are:

Month	Number of Visitors
June	11,764
July	22,164
August	25,818

380
738
59,746.00
832

The peak visiting hours are estimated by the Park Rangers to be the same as for Sand Point or at Miner's Castle.

ICE CREAM/FOOD COSTS

Mr. Snedeker estimates that the following figures pertain to his cost of goods sold for each dollar of sales.

	Ice Cream	Food
Sales	$1.00	$1.00
Cost of goods sold	0.50	0.60
Gross Margin	$0.50	$0.40

COSTS OF A TRUCK

Mr. Snedeker attempted to estimate what it might cost to buy and operate a truck to sell Hasty Tasty products. Renting/leasing was considered but ruled out to the specialized needs (e.g., service counter, heating equipment, refrigeration equipment, awning, etc.) of the truck. Since the actual acquisition costs would in large part be a function of the amount of time devoted to "shopping around," a best case/worst case scenario was developed. It is as follows:

Item	Best Case	Worst Case
Truck	$3,000.00	$8,000.00
Equipment	3,000.00	4,000.00
Awning, Lights, Paint	200.00	500.00

Item	Best Case	Worst Case
Modification for Truck		
(window, counter, etc.)	100.00	400.00
Insurance	300.00	400.00
Licenses (food, truck, etc.)	10.00	200.00
Total	$6,700.00	$13,500.00
Other:		
Driver	$4.28/hr.	$4.28/hr.
Gasoline/Oil Maintenance	0.25/mile	0.30/mile
Propane/Electricity	0.30/hr.	0.50/hr.

The Snedekers wondered if they should buy and remodel a truck. If so, which site would be the most profitable for them? Should they start selling at both sites, and if so, would they need two trucks?

Introduction to How Worksheets are Setup

All the worksheets in this manual follow a common outline and do not assume you have used other worksheets in the manual. Read over the following material describing how to use the SAMPLE worksheet. Experienced users should have no problem following the instructions. Users without Microsoft Excel or Lotus 1-2-3 experience should look over the remaining material in this chapter and then read the next chapter "Introduction to Spreadsheets" before attempting to work the SAMPLE worksheet.

How to Use the Worksheet

If you have no experience with Microsoft Excel or Lotus 1-2-3 read this section without actually loading the program, and continue on to the next Chapter entitled, "Introduction to Spreadsheets."

1.   Fill out the input form provided for this worksheet after reading the case.

2.   If you have not used any of the worksheets in this manual, please review the section of the manual on how to load Microsoft Excel, Lotus 1-2-3 or a compatible program and the worksheets provided on the disk.

3.   Load the spreadsheet program: Microsoft Excel, Lotus 1-2-3, or a compatible program. After a blank spreadsheet, load the worksheet using the keystrokes shown in the table below. See the section of the manual on how to load worksheets if you experience difficulties.

Keystrokes for Excel or 1-2-3W	Comments
ALT FO	Access the Command menu, the File menu and execute the Retrieve command.
SAMPLE	Either type in the file name, or highlight the name using the cursor keys, or mouse.
ENTER	Press the Enter key to load the worksheet.

Table 2-1:   Load SAMPLE worksheet

4.   After loading the worksheet, review it to make sure you know where the input cells are located. The input cells are colored differently than the rest of the cells on a color monitor. The first time you use the worksheet, most of the cells in the spreadsheet will display "#NA" or "NA", but don't worry. As you enter your inputs, the "NA" shown in output cells will be replaced by calculated values. Excel worksheets show "#NA", and 1-2-3 for Windows show "NA."

Each input cell is boxed for emphasis in the figure below. Unless you have disabled the worksheet protection, only the input cells can be changed. If you accidentally attempt to change a protected (non-input) cell, the program will display an error message on the screen. You may need to press the **ESC** or **ENTER** key to return to normal operations.

Spreadsheet Screen

	A	B	C	D
1	**Name = SAMPLE**			
2				
3	**Sample Case - Hasty Tasty**			
4		**Best**	**Worst**	
5	**Enter Inputs Below:**	**Case**	**Case**	
6	**Sales:**			
7	Average Daily Sales	#N/A	#N/A	/Day
8	No. of Days Operated During Summer	#N/A	#N/A	Days
9	**Variable Costs:**			
10	Cost of Goods Sold (as % of Sales)	#N/A	#N/A	%
11	**Operating Expenses:**			
12	Truck & Equipment Depreciation	#N/A	#N/A	/yr.
13	Insurance	#N/A	#N/A	/yr.
14	Licenses	#N/A	#N/A	/yr.
15	**Other:**			
16	Hours Open per Day	#N/A	#N/A	Hrs/Day
17	Driver Cost per Hour	#N/A	#N/A	/Hr.
18	Propane & Electric Cost per Hour	#N/A	#N/A	/Hr.
19	Miles Driven per Day	#N/A	#N/A	Miles/Day
20	Gasoline/Oil Maintenance per Mile	#N/A	#N/A	/Mile
21				

Figure 2-1:   Input area of worksheet

5.   Type into the spreadsheet your estimates of the inputs using the information from the input forms you filled out in Step 1. Use the cursor keys ⬅, ➡, ⬇, and ⬆ to move to the desired cell location. Type the number and press the ⏎ key or one of the cursor keys. Repeat this procedure until all the necessary input cells are filled.

Viewing The Spreadsheet Calculations

You can press the cursor keys (⬅, ➡, ⬇, and ⬆), or the Page Up, PG↑, and the Page Down, PG↓, keys to move around the worksheet area. You need to set the Transition Navigation Keys option in Excel return to cell A1 by pressing the HOME key, else you must press CTRL HOME.

If you want to see portions of both the inputs and the calculated results at the same time, you can open up a horizontal window using the Vertical Split Bar. Use the Horizontal Split Bar to create a vertical separation. See Chapter 3, Introduction to Spreadsheets for more information.

Saving the Spreadsheet

After entering your estimates and examining the results, including the graph, save your spreadsheet by using the following commands. The first keystroke column contains the commands for either Microsoft Excel, or Lotus 1-2-3 for Windows.

Keystrokes for Excel or 1-2-3W	Comments
ESC ESC	If the top of the display screen shows one of the command menus, (see the introduction section of the manual) press the Escape key until the menus disappear. Skip this step if a menu is not displayed.
ALT FS	Access the Command menu, the File menu and the Save option.
ENTER	Press Enter to save under the same name. An Excel file is saved with a "XLS" suffix, and a 1-2-3 for Windows file is saved as a "WK4" file.

Table 2-2:   Save worksheet.

Printing The Worksheet

Select the worksheet containing the analysis, place the mouse cursor on top of the "Print Worksheet" button and click on the left-mouse button to print it. Select the worksheet containing the graph, and click on the "Print Chart" button to print the graph. Make sure you have a printer connected and turned on before attempting to print your results.

See the introduction to the manual for additional information on printing if you have difficulty and for information on printing a graph. Bring the results of your analysis to class when the case is discussed.

Input Form for Sample Case - Hasty Tasty

Name : _____

```
              Sample Case - Hasty Tasty
                        Best        Worst
                        Case        Case
                     _____   _____

Sales:

Average Daily Sales                               /Day

No. of Days Operated During Summer                Days

Variable Costs:

Cost of Goods Sold (as % of Sales)                %

Operating Expenses:

Truck & Equipment Depreciation                    /yr.

Insurance                                         /yr.

Licenses                                          /yr.

Hours Open per Day                                Hrs/Day

Driver Cost per Hour                              /Hr.

Propane & Electric Cost per Hour                  /Hr.

Miles Driven per Day                              Miles/Day

Gasoline/Oil Maintenance per Mile                 /Mile
```

Output Form for Sample Case - Hasty Tasty

Name _____

```
          Hasty Tasty Pro Forma Income Statements
                              Best        Worst
                              Case        Case

                          _____  _____

Sales                     _____  _____

Cost of Goods Sold        _____  _____

Gross Profit              _____  _____

   Operating Expenses:    _____  _____

   Wages                  _____  _____

   Depreciation           _____  _____

   Gasoline & Oil         _____  _____

   Propane & Electricity  _____  _____

   Insurance              _____  _____

   Licenses               _____  _____

Total Expenses:           _____  _____

Net Income or Loss        _____  _____
```

CHAPTER 3:
Introduction to Spreadsheets

Introduction

If you are familiar with Microsoft Excel or Lotus 1-2-3 for Windows then you may want to simply review this chapter of the manual. However, if you have no experience with a spreadsheet program, then you should carefully read this chapter.

This introductory chapter discusses how to:

- turn on the computer
- run Microsoft Excel or Lotus 1-2-3 for Windows
- load the worksheets supplied in this manual
- enter information into the worksheets
- see graphs of key values in the worksheets
- print the worksheets
- save your analysis
- exit from Microsoft Excel or Lotus 1-2-3 for Windows

These instructions use a sample case, Hasty Tasty, as a basis for explaining the use of Microsoft Excel or Lotus 1-2-3 for Windows in case analysis. If you have not already read the sample case in Chapter 2, then please read it before you continue.

After you read the case, please fill out the form named "Input Form for Sample Case - Hasty Tasty" in Chapter 2. By using this form you can record the key input estimates as you read the case and be ready to enter the information when you work with the spreadsheet program.

Computer Lab Procedures

Some computer center labs keep their IBM (or other compatible) personal computers (PCs) turned on continuously, and/or have special procedures students should use to load programs. Please check with your computer lab concerning the procedures to begin operations. However, if you are using a personal computer that is not connected to a network or any other computer, then the following instructions apply.

Make sure you have all the information for your case ready to enter because sometimes the computer center or computer lab is being used to capacity and you may only have a limited amount of time on the machine. Plan ahead and select a time when your computer center is not busy.

Locate a personal computer that is not being used and examine it before continuing. The computer has three main components: a monitor, a keyboard, and a system box. The system box is what the monitor is often sitting on and contains the actual computer components and the floppy disk drives. Some system boxes are contained in a self-standing unit called a tower. See Figure 3-1 for an example of a tower unit. Check to see if a printer is attached and turn it on if you plan to print out your results.

Location of Disk Drives

Identify the "A" disk drive. The computer may have one or two disk drives located either horizontally or vertically as shown in Figure 3-1. On horizontally mounted disk drives, the left-hand drive is usually designated as the "A" drive. On vertically mounted disk drives the top disk drive is usually the "A" drive. However, if you have a question about the location of the "A" drive, please check with the computer lab personnel. If there is only one floppy disk drive, it is the "A" disk drive.

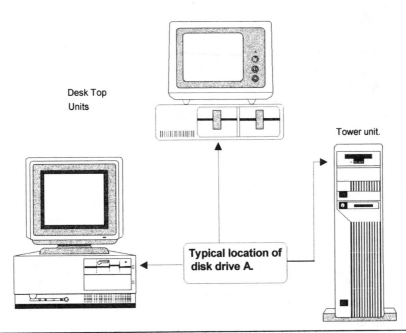

Desk Top Units

Tower unit.

Typical location of disk drive A.

Figure 3-1:   Location of Disk Drives

Floppy disks

5 1/4" Disks

A 5 1/4" DOS disk is usually inside a protective paper sleeve. Don't confuse the protective sleeve with the square heavy paper that completely encloses the disk. The label on the disk should always be on the top side as shown in Figure 3-2 below. Please notice that the front of the disk has two small notches as well as an oval shaped opening. The square opening on the side of the disk is the "write protect notch" and must not be covered if you want to save your worksheet results. When handling a disk, do not bend it or touch any of its exposed parts because these actions can damage the information contained on the disk. When the disk is not being used, keep it inside the protective sleeve.

Before inserting a 5 1/4" disk into a disk drive, remove the disk from the protective paper sleeve, make sure that the label is facing upward, the write protect notch is to your left, and the oval opening is facing forward.

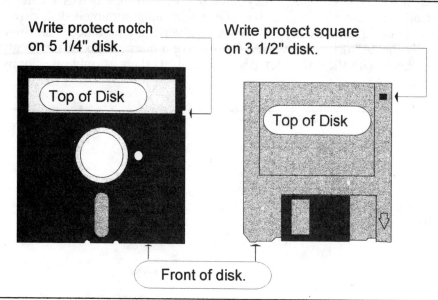

Figure 3-2:   Types of Floppy Disks

3 1/2" Disks:

A 3 1/2" disk has the label on the top and has a metal opening on the front edge of the disk. Make sure that the label is facing upward and the metal opening facing forward before inserting the disk in a disk drive. A 3 1/2" disk has either one or two rectangular slots on the sides of the disk. One slot contains a sliding switch. This is the write protect mechanism. You push a sliding switch that either fills the slot or leaves it empty. When the switch fills the slot you can write to the disk but, if the slot is empty, you cannot write to the disk. If the disk has only one slot, then it is a double density (760K) disk. High-density (1.44 MB) 3 1/2" disks have a second rectangular slot on the disk.

How to Turn on a Computer That has a Hard Disk

Make sure the "A" disk drive door is open if the computer has a "hard disk". Ask the lab personnel if you are not sure whether or not the machine has a hard disk. Desktop computers have an "ON/OFF" switch usually on the back or toward the rear right hand side of the machine as shown in Figure 3-3. Tower units normally have a switch on the front of the unit. Turn on the computer and, if necessary, turn on the monitor. Please check with the lab personnel about the need for turning on the monitor.

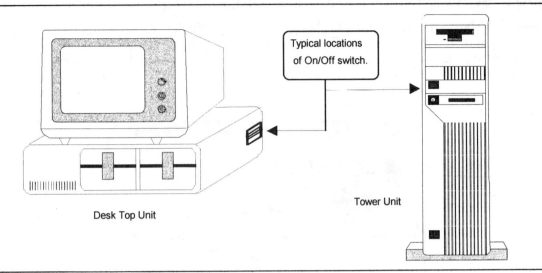

Figure 3-3:   ON/OFF Switch location

Start Windows Program

If you are using Microsoft Excel, then read the material below. After you turn on the computer, you must start Microsoft Windows before you can use a window program. If the Windows program is not executing, then type the following at the DOS prompt.

C:> WIN

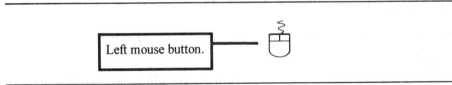

Figure 3-4:   Two Button Mouse

In Microsoft Windows based programs, you use both the mouse and the cursor keys to make menu selections and to move about the screen. You select menu items by using the mouse to place the cursor on a selection, and clicking either once or twice with the "Left" mouse button.

Figure 3-4 shows a two-button mouse. If your system has a three-button mouse, you still press the left mouse button for selections. After the windows program loads, you should see either an icon called "Program Manager", or an open window called "Program Manager" if you are using Windows 3.1. Windows 95 users will see a taskbar on the screen..

Microsoft Specific Instructions

This section of the text gets you started on using Microsoft Excel for Windows. If you are using Lotus 1-2-3 for Windows, then turn to that section.

How to Start Microsoft Excel in Windows 3.1

Figure 3-5 shows the Microsoft Excel program in the "WinApps" program group, but on your computer screen it may be in an "Excel" program group or in another program group. Place the cursor on the program group icon that contains the Microsoft Excel program and double click with the left mouse button to open up the window.

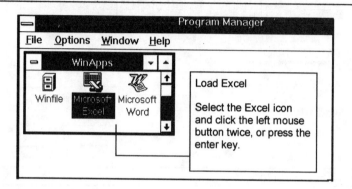

Figure 3-5:   Selecting Excel Icon

How to Start Microsoft Excel in Windows 95

Figure 3-6 shows one method for starting Excel in Windows 95. Press the Start button on the Task Bar. Select Programs from the start menu and then select Microsoft Excel from the program menu. You may also have an icon for the program showing on the desktop that you can click-on to start the program.

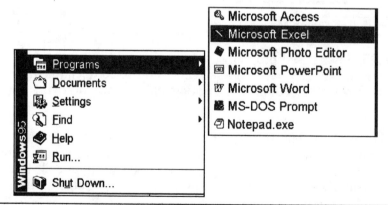

Figure 3-6:   Starting Microsoft Excel in Windows 95

After you load the Microsoft Excel program, the spreadsheet should match that in Figure 3-7. This book shows the screens for Microsoft Excel 97, however all files in this book will operate correctly in Microsoft Version 5.0.

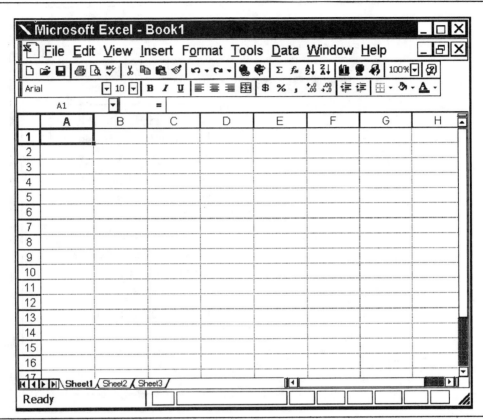

Figure 3-7:   Excel Worksheet Screen

Accessing Menus with Keystrokes

Microsoft Excel provides you with several options for executing commands in the program. Using the mouse to select menu items or to click on special icons is one approach. The second method is using keystrokes to select menu items.

When you access a Microsoft Excel menu, many of the menu options have a letter underlined. The underlined letter means that that menu option can be chosen by holding down the ⟦ALT⟧ key and pressing the letter key with the underline. For example, "⟦ALT⟧ F" displays the File menu on the screen, and the menu option "Open" has an underline under the letter "O." Therefore, you can either use the mouse to select the menu items, or you can use the keystrokes "⟦ALT⟧ FO" to access them. In this book, the keystroke tables show the ⟦ALT⟧ letter combinations. After you work with the worksheet commands, you will start using the mouse instead of the keystrokes, but the keystroke tables are excellent for users that have no experience with Microsoft Excel.

Open Worksheet File Menu

The first two steps in opening the file are shown in the following figure. Select the File menu option, and then the Open menu option. The keystrokes to execute the menu commands shown in the Figure 3-8 are: "[ALT] FO."

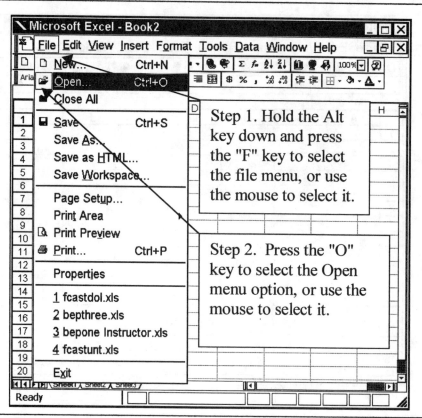

Figure 3-8:   Excel Worksheet Screen

Set Disk Drive and Load Worksheet

After you select the Open menu option, the Open window appears, and you select the disk drive containing the files, and load the SAMPLE.XLS template. The keystrokes are shown in Table 3-1 below.

Keystrokes	Comments
[ALT] I	Select the Drives option.
	Use the cursor key or mouse to select the drive where your files are located. You probably have the file on the disk in Drive A.
[ENTER]	Press Enter to open the file, or double click with the left mouse button.

Table 3-1:   Load a file in Microsoft Excel

The following figure shows the Open menu with explanations on how to open the files. You normally use the mouse to make the selections by highlighting the menu choices and clicking on them with the left mouse button.

If you have copied the worksheet files onto the hard disk, then execute "[ALT] I" and select the directory containing the files. Next use the mouse to scroll the list of names in the file name box, and then select the file by clicking on it. (See Figure 3-9.)

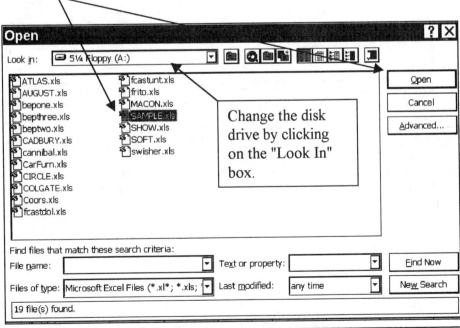

Figure 3-9:   Selecting the Excel Worksheet File

After you load the worksheet, the computer monitor should display the spreadsheet shown in Figure 3-10.

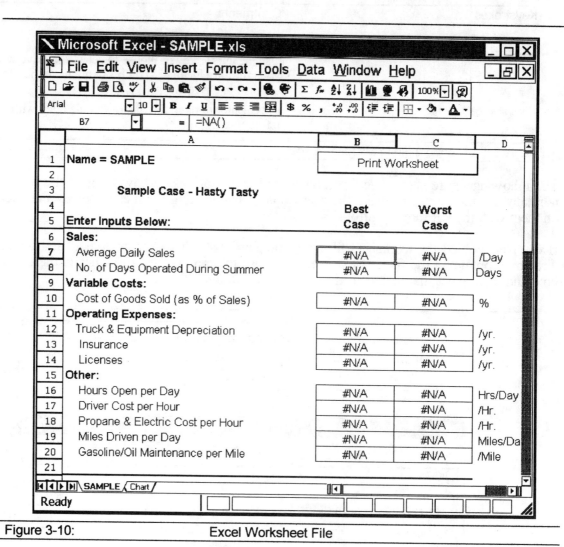

Figure 3-10:   Excel Worksheet File

The cursor is located on cell B7 where you begin entering input numbers. The "#N/A" is displayed for many cells in the worksheet, but as you enter the inputs, the "#N/As" will disappear.

How to Save the Microsoft Excel Spreadsheet

You save the Microsoft Excel spreadsheet by selecting the File menu and the Save option. You save the files in the "XLS" format. The keystroke tables in this book assume you retain the "XLS" format. Table 3-5 walks you through saving the file.

Keystrokes	Comments
[ALT] F	Select the File menu.
S	Select the save menu choice.

Table 3-2:   Save a file in Microsoft Excel

How to Exit Microsoft Excel

You exit from Microsoft Excel by selecting the File menu, and the Exit option. If you have not saved the current worksheet, the program will ask you if you want to save it before you exit Excel.

Keystrokes	Comments
[ALT] F	Select the File menu.
X	Select the Exit menu choice.

Table 3-3:   Exit Excel

Set Navigation Keys Option

When using the worksheets in this book make sure you set the Navigation Keys option. This option makes the program treat the navigation keys, Home, End, etc., the same as the Lotus 1-2-3 program. The menu location and procedure for both Versions 5 and 97 of Excel is:

> Select Tools Menu
> Select Options
> Select Transition Navigation Keys
> Turn on option

Lotus 1-2-3 Specific Instructions

This section of the text gets you started on using Lotus 1-2-3 for Windows. The examples in this book use Lotus 1-2-3 Release 5.0, but if you are using later version of the program, the commands for loading and saving spreadsheets should not differ between versions.

How to Start Lotus 1-2-3 in Windows

First make sure the computer you are using has the program installed on it. If you are using Windows 3.1, then open the Program Manager and locate the program group that contains the 1-2-3 program, and then click on the program icon. If you are using Windows 95, then click on the Start button on the Task Bar and select the "Programs" menu option. You then select the Lotus 1-2-3 program from the list displayed on the screen.

After you load the Lotus 1-2-3 program the spreadsheet should be similar to that in the next figure. This book shows the screens for Lotus 1-2-3 Release 5.0, however all files will work with later versions of the program.

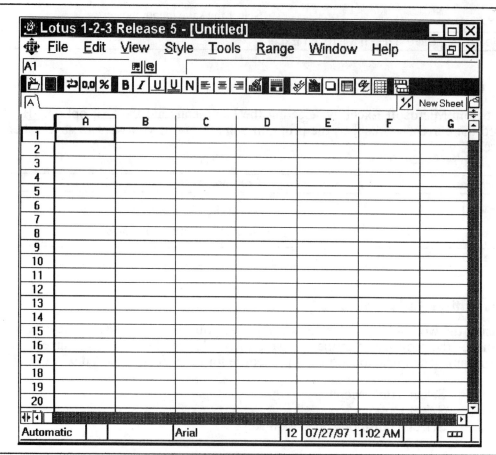

Figure 3-11   Lotus 1-2-3 Worksheet File

Accessing Menus with Keystrokes

Lotus 1-2-3 provides you with several options for executing commands in the program. Using the mouse to select menu items or to click on special icons is one approach. The second method is using keystrokes to select menu items.

When you access a Lotus 1-2-3 menu, many of the menu options have a letter underlined. The underlined letter means that that menu option can be chosen by holding down the [ALT] key and pressing the letter key with the underline. For example, "[ALT] F" displays the File menu on the screen, and the menu option "Open" has an underline under the letter "O." Therefore, you can either use the mouse to select the menu items, or you can use the keystrokes "[ALT] FO" to access them. In this book, the keystroke tables show the [ALT] letter combinations. After you work with the worksheet commands, you will start using the mouse instead of the keystrokes, but the keystroke tables are excellent for users that have no experience with Lotus 1-2-3.

Open Worksheet File Menu

The first two steps in opening the file are shown in the following figure. Select the File menu option, and then the Open menu option. The keystrokes to execute the menu commands shown in Figure 3-12 are: "[ALT] FO."

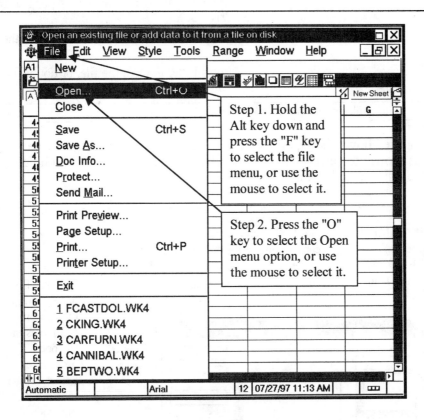

| Figure 3-12 | Lotus 1-2-3 Worksheet Screen |

Set Disk Drive and Load Worksheet

After you select the Open menu option, the Open window appears, and you select the disk drive containing the files, and load the SAMPLE.WK4 template. The keystrokes are shown in Table 3-4 below.

Keystrokes	Comments
ALT V	Select the Drives option.
A	Enter A if the disk is in drive A, or B if the disk is in drive B.
	Use the cursor key or mouse to select the SAMPLE file.
ENTER	Press Enter to open the file, or double click with the left mouse button.

Table 3-4:   Load a file in Lotus 1-2-3

The following figure shows the Open menu with explanations on how to open the files. You normally use the mouse to select the selections by highlighting the menu choices and clicking on them with the left mouse button.

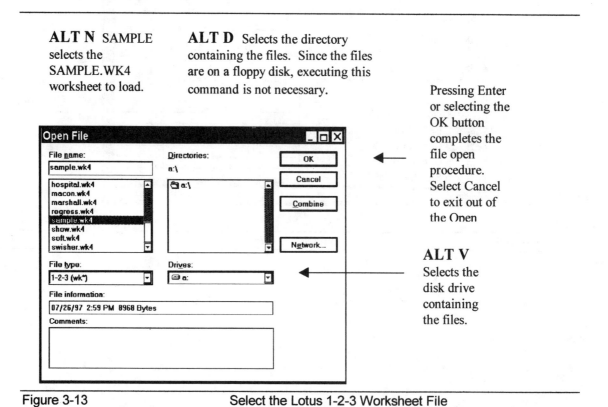

ALT N SAMPLE selects the SAMPLE.WK4 worksheet to load.

ALT D Selects the directory containing the files. Since the files are on a floppy disk, executing this command is not necessary.

Pressing Enter or selecting the OK button completes the file open procedure. Select Cancel to exit out of the Open

ALT V Selects the disk drive containing the files.

Figure 3-13   Select the Lotus 1-2-3 Worksheet File

After you load the worksheet, the computer screen should display a worksheet similar to the one in the next figure.

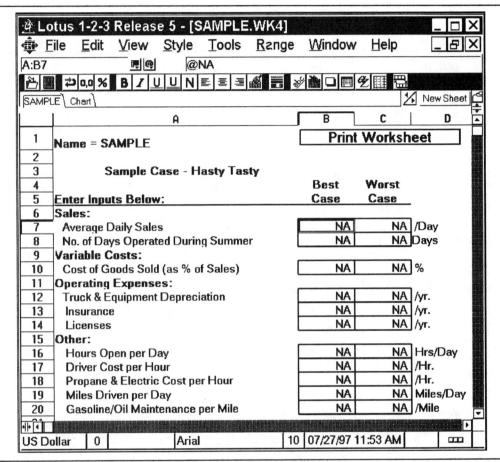

Figure 3-14   Lotus 1-2-3 Worksheet Screen

The cursor is located on cell B7 where you begin entering input numbers. The "NA" is displayed for many cells in the worksheet, but as you enter the inputs, the "NA" text will disappear.

How to Save the Lotus 1-2-3 Spreadsheet

You save the Lotus 1-2-3 spreadsheet by selecting the File menu and the Save option. You save the files in the "WK4" format. The keystroke tables in this book assume you retain the "WK4" format. Table 3-XX walks you through saving the file.

Keystrokes	Comments
ALT F	Select the File menu.
S	Select the save menu choice.

Table 3-5:   Save a file in Lotus 1-2-3

How to Exit Lotus 1-2-3

You exit from Lotus 1-2-3 by selecting the File menu, and the Exit option. If you have not saved the current worksheet, the program will ask you if you want to save it before you exit Lotus 1-2-3.

Keystrokes	Comments
[ALT] F	Select the File menu.
X	Select the Exit menu choice.

Table 3-6:	Exit Lotus 1-2-3

Spreadsheet Techniques Common to Lotus 1-2-3 and Microsoft Excel

The remaining material in this chapter discusses spreadsheet techniques which are similar for both Microsoft and Lotus 1-2-3 Excel, and unless otherwise noted the following material applies to both spreadsheet programs.

Using the Keyboard Keys with a Spreadsheet

Figure 3-15 shows two common styles of PC keyboards. The keys are arranged much the same as a standard typewriter keyboard. The top row includes the number keys with the alphabetic keys contained in the next three rows. The space bar is the long key at the bottom and the Shift keys are on either side of it. Press either of the Shift keys to access the alternative letter or symbol on keys, or to change the case (upper or lower) on alphabetic keys.

The four cursor keys ([←], [→], [↓], and [↑]) are used to move the cursor around the Lotus worksheet. The cursor key arrow points in the direction the cursor will move once you press the key.

On the early IBM PC/AT keyboard style, the key grouping on the right hand side of the keyboard is defaulted to the cursor key mode. When the computer is turned on, the keys act as cursor keys. You can change the key grouping to the ten-key number pad mode by pressing the Num Lock key. This key is a toggle switch, so after turning on the ten-key mode, pressing the key a second time returns to the cursor key mode. You can temporarily change the mode by holding down the Shift key while pressing the cursor keys. It is probably easier to use the key grouping on the right as a cursor pad, and use the top row of keys for entering numbers with this keyboard.

There are two sets of cursor keys on the current style keyboard. The number grouping on the far right side of the keyboard is set as a ten key pad for entering numbers when the computer is turned on. The middle group of four keys are used as cursor keys. When the Number Lock [Num Lock] key is pressed or active, the key group on the right acts as a ten key pad. If the key is not active, then the keys are cursor keys. Most keyboards have a light that indicates when the [Num Lock] key is on.

The Page Up [PG↑] key moves the cursor up 20 lines when pressed. The Page Down [PG↓] key moves the cursor down 20 lines.

The [END] key moves the cursor back to Cell A1 when pressed. The Tab, [TAB], key moves the cursor to the right one screen at a time. The combination of [SHIFT] [TAB] moves the screen to the left.

The function keys grouped either on the right hand side or on the top of the keyboard have special uses in Lotus. You will use some of these function keys with the templates in this manual.

Locate the [ESC] key, which is normally on the upper left or right-hand side of the keyboard. This is your "get out of trouble" key. Press the [ESC] key when you want to get out of a menu or cancel an entry you made in the worksheet.

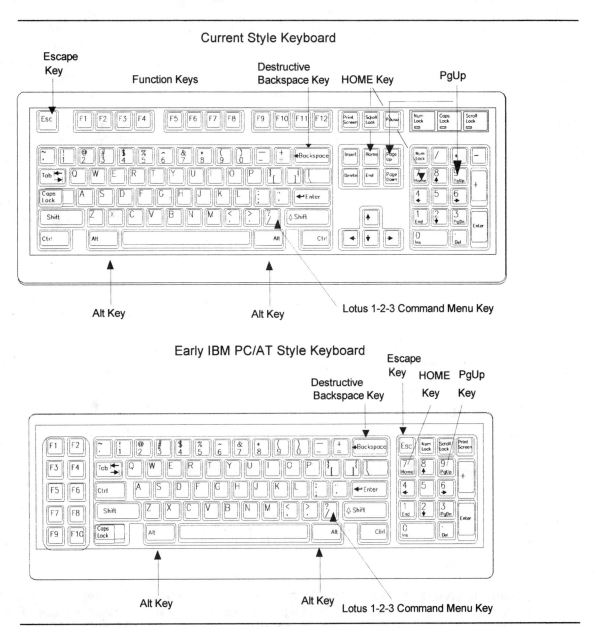

Figure 3-15:   PC Keyboards

Spreadsheet Data Entry

You enter numbers into a worksheet by moving the cursor to the desired location and typing in the numbers. After you type the numbers press either the [ENTER] key or one of the cursor keys to place the number in the cell. For example, move the cursor to an empty cell and type 345.67 [ENTER]. Look at the screen and then look at the cell indicator in the upper left-hand corner of the window. The cell indicator shows the cursor location, and the contents of the cell, which in this case is a number.

You can enter text beginning with the letters "A" to "Z" (lower or upper case) by typing in the characters and pressing either the [ENTER] key or a cursor key. For example, move the cursor to an empty cell and type in "HELLO", and press the [ENTER] key. Then examine the cell indicator in the upper left-hand corner of the display. You should see the cell location and " 'HELLO". The single quote means the text is left justified in the cell. You do not type the single quote. When the first alphabetic key is pressed, the program automatically inserts a single quote, " ' ", before the first character. You center text by typing a caret "^" as the first character. You right justify text by typing a double quote ' " ' as the first character. You can also use the worksheet menus to format text. You center numbers using the programs format menu.

When you enter information that is text, but begins with a number such as a telephone number, then type one of the following three characters before entering the number " ' ^ " ". For example, you enter a centered telephone number by placing the "^" character in front of the first integer, e.g., ^555-1200.

For practice move the cursor to an empty cell and type in the following three words in different cells. Examine the cell indicator window and the displayed text on the screen for each entry.

Type	Result
'SEE	Left-justified text.
^THE	Centered text.
"TREE	Right-justified text.

Simple Equations

The spreadsheet programs use the following arithmetic symbols:

+	Add	( )	Parentheses
-	Subtract	-	Negative sign
*	Multiply	^	Exponential
/	Division		

The programs reference spreadsheet cells by Column and Row. Because the Column references are alphabetic characters (A, B..IV), you must put a math operator in front of the reference. For example, place the number 10 in Cell A1 and the number 25 in Cell A2. In cell A3 enter the equation +A1*A2, and watch 250 appear on the screen. In the upper left-hand corner of the screen you see the equation.

You must place one of the math operators in front of the first cell address. Each worksheet cell is a little calculator. Move your cursor to an empty cell and type in the following: +3+5+10   [ENTER]

After you press the Enter key look at the cell indicator in the upper left-hand corner of the window. It displays the cell location and the equation you typed in. The worksheet screen displays the results of the equation.

Now type in the following equations in different cells. Examine the results on the screen and the cell's content in the indicator window.

5^2	[ENTER]	Square a number.
36^.5	[ENTER]	Square root of a number.
(5+12+56)/23	[ENTER]	Division
(6+4)*(3+7)	[ENTER]	Multiplication

If you make a mistake, just type over the cell with the corrected values.

Function Keys

The group of 12 function keys on the top of the current style keyboards or the 10 function keys on the left-hand side of the older keyboards have special meanings in Microsoft Excel and Lotus 1-2-3. While you will not work with all the function keys in this manual, you will use several. These keys are:

[F1]	Help Key.	Press to get help.
[F2]	Edit Key.	Press to edit contents of cell under cursor.
[F5]	Go to Key.	Press and enter cell address to move the cursor to a specified cell. To move to cell A10, press [F5]A10[ENTER].

Each of these keys is discussed in this chapter.

Keystroke Tables

Rather than attempting to show figures of all the command menus in this manual, the remainder of the book uses keystroke tables. Assuming you still have some of the equations and text examples showing on the screen, the following table's keystrokes will erase the worksheet from computer memory, but not from the disk.

The first column contains the keystrokes for <u>Microsoft Excel and Lotus 1-2-3</u>. If there are differences then two columns of keystrokes are shown. The right-most column contains brief comments. Please make sure you are not in the middle of a menu when you press the command key. Always look at the top of the screen before you begin executing the commands in a table. If you are in a menu, just press the [ESC] key until the menu disappears.

Clear Worksheet Screen

You clear the screen by closing the file or opening a second worksheet. In this book, we assume you work with the worksheets one at a time. If you want to save the results, then answer "Yes" when prompted by the program.

Keystrokes for Excel or 1-2-3W	Comments
[ALT] F	Access the File menu.
C	Select the Close menu option using the cursor keys, or mouse.
Y	Select the Yes option if you want to save the current file.

Table 3-7:   Close Worksheet

SAMPLE.WK1 Worksheet Example

This example assumes you have an "A" and a "B" disk drive on your computer. Place the disk that came with this manual into the "A" disk drive and close the disk drive door. Make sure the disk drive does not contain a disk before you insert your disk.

After you set the program to read from the drive containing the disk with the worksheet files, you are ready to load it into computer memory. Table 3-8, "Load SAMPLE Worksheet", shows you how to load the Hasty Tasty worksheet named SAMPLE.

Keystrokes for Excel or 1-2-3W	Comments
[ALT] FO	Access the Command menu, the File menu and execute the Retrieve command.
SAMPLE	Either type in the file name, or highlight the name using the cursor keys, or mouse.
[ENTER]	Press the Enter key to load the worksheet.

Table 3-8:   Load File

After you load the SAMPLE worksheet your computer display should be similar to the one in the next figure.

Worksheet Screen

	A	B	C	D
1	**Name = SAMPLE**			
2				
3	**Sample Case - Hasty Tasty**			
4		**Best**	**Worst**	
5	**Enter Inputs Below:**	**Case**	**Case**	
6	**Sales:**			
7	Average Daily Sales	#N/A	#N/A	/Day
8	No. of Days Operated During Summer	#N/A	#N/A	Days
9	**Variable Costs:**			
10	Cost of Goods Sold (as % of Sales)	#N/A	#N/A	%
11	**Operating Expenses:**			
12	Truck & Equipment Depreciation	#N/A	#N/A	/yr.
13	Insurance	#N/A	#N/A	/yr.
14	Licenses	#N/A	#N/A	/yr.
15	**Other:**			
16	Hours Open per Day	#N/A	#N/A	Hrs/Day
17	Driver Cost per Hour	#N/A	#N/A	/Hr.
18	Propane & Electric Cost per Hour	#N/A	#N/A	/Hr.
19	Miles Driven per Day	#N/A	#N/A	Miles/Day
20	Gasoline/Oil Maintenance per Mile	#N/A	#N/A	/Mile
21				

Figure 3-16:   Input area of worksheet.

How to Enter Data Into the Worksheet

You can change only those cells that are unprotected in the worksheets accompanying this manual. You cannot accidentally overwrite a cell containing an equation. If you accidentally attempt to change a protected (non-input) cell, the program will display an error message box on the screen. Press the [ESC] key to return to normal operations.

After loading the worksheet, review it to make sure you know where the input cells are located. The input cells are colored differently than the rest of the cells on a color monitor. They have a brighter intensity than the other cells on a monochrome (black and white) monitor. Also, the first time you use the worksheet, most of the cells in the spreadsheet will display "#NA" or, "NA", but don't worry. As you enter your values in the input cells, the NA's in the output cells are replaced by calculated values.

Assuming you have read and studied the case, your input form should be similar to that shown in the next figure named "Completed Hasty Tasty Input Form."

```
Input Form for Sample Case - Hasty Tasty
Name     J. Market
                    Sample Case - Hasty Tasty
                                        Best        Worst
                                        Case        Case


Sales:
Average Daily Sales                     300         250         /Day
No. of Days Operated During Summer       85          80         Days
Variable Costs:
Cost of Goods Sold (as % of Sales)       54          54         %
Operating Expenses:
Truck & Equipment Depreciation         2100        4300         /yr.
Insurance                               300         400         /yr.
Licenses                                100         200         /yr.
Hours Open per Day                        8           9         Hrs/Day
Driver Cost per Hour                    4.28        4.28        /Hr.
Propane & Electric Cost per Hour        .30         .50         /Hr.
Miles Driven per Day                     22          22         Miles/Day
Gasoline/Oil Maintenance per Mile       .25         .30         /Mile
```

Figure 3-17   Completed Hasty Tasty Input Form

Type Values in Spreadsheet From Input Form

Move the cursor to the appropriate cell and type in the values from the input sheet. If you make a mistake while typing an input, press the [ENTER] key and then just type over the old entry. Note, the letter "O" cannot be used in place of "0" (Zero), nor can the lower case letter "l" replace the "1" (One) in a number. After you enter the numbers, your display screen should match Figure 3-18.

Worksheet Screen

	A	B	C	D
1	Name = SAMPLE	Print Worksheet		
2				
3	Sample Case - Hasty Tasty			
4		Best	Worst	
5	Enter Inputs Below:	Case	Case	
6	Sales:			
7	Average Daily Sales	$300	$250	/Day
8	No. of Days Operated During Summer	85	80	Days
9	Variable Costs:			
10	Cost of Goods Sold (as % of Sales)	54.00	54.00	%
11	Operating Expenses:			
12	Truck & Equipment Depreciation	$2,100.00	$4,300.00	/yr.
13	Insurance	$300.00	$400.00	/yr.
14	Licenses	$100.00	$200.00	/yr.
15	Other:			
16	Hours Open per Day	8.00	9.00	Hrs/Day
17	Driver Cost per Hour	$4.28	$4.28	/Hr.
18	Propane & Electric Cost per Hour	$0.30	$0.50	/Hr.
19	Miles Driven per Day	22.00	22.00	Miles/Day
20	Gasoline/Oil Maintenance per Mile	$0.25	$0.30	/Mile
21				
22				

SAMPLE / Chart /

Figure 3-17: SAMPLE worksheet with inputs

As you typed in the numbers, the "NA" symbols disappeared and were replaced by the entered values. The worksheet automatically formats the values. You don't type in the commas between thousands or the "$" dollar signs, the program formats the displayed values.

Examine Reports

You can use the mouse to move about the spreadsheet, or you can use the keys. Press the [PG↓] key once to move down 20 rows or [PG↑] to move up 20 rows. You can also use the [↓] cursor key to move down the worksheet, but it takes longer. The [PG↓] and [PG↑] keys are the fastest for moving a screen full of lines. Use the cursor keys to position the report on your screen to match 3-19.

Worksheet Screen

	A	B	C	D
24				
25	PRO FORMA INCOME STATEMENTS	**Best**	**Worst**	
26		**Case**	**Case**	
27				
28	Sales	$25,500	$20,000	
29	Cost of Goods Sold	13,770	10,800	
30				
31	Gross Profit	$11,730	$9,200	
32				
33	Operating Expenses:			
34	Wages	$2,910	$3,082	
35	Depreciation	2,100	4,300	
36	Gasoline & Oil	468	528	
37	Propane & Electricity	204	360	
38	Insurance	300	400	
39	Licenses	100	200	
40				
41	Total Operating Expenses	$6,082	$8,870	
42				
43	Net Income or Loss	$5,648	$330	

SAMPLE / Chart /

Figure 3-19   Sample report

Save the Worksheet Results

You save the worksheet with your inputs using the File Save menu command. Table 3-9, "Saving the Worksheet" contains the keystrokes for saving the file with the same name. After entering your estimates and examining the results, including the graph, save your spreadsheet by using the following commands.

Keystrokes for Excel or 1-2-3W	Comments
[ESC] [ESC]	If the top of the display screen shows one of the command menus, (see the introduction section of the manual) press the Escape key until the menus disappear. Skip this step if a menu is not displayed.
[ALT] FS	Access the Command menu, the File menu and the Save option.
[ENTER]	Press Enter to save under the same name. An Excel file is saved with a "XLS" suffix, and a 1-2-3 for Windows file is saved as a "WK4" file.

Table 3-9:   Save SAMPLE worksheet

Macros in Case Worksheets

The worksheet files in this manual uses "Macros" for printing the results. In Lotus 1-2-3 a macro is text containing commands, while in Microsoft Excel a macro is Visual Basic for Applications code that the spreadsheet program executes. You execute macros by using a "Control + Key" combination, or by clicking on a graphical object such as a button.

How to Print a Worksheet With Macro Command

All of the spreadsheets in this book have a "Print Button" at the top of the model. You double click on the Print Spreadsheet button with the left mouse button to print the spreadsheet.

How to Split the Windows in the Worksheet

You can divide the worksheet screen into two windows by placing the mouse pointer on either the vertical or horizontal spit bars. The following figure shows the location of the split bars in each type of spreadsheet.

Worksheet Screen

Excel Screen:

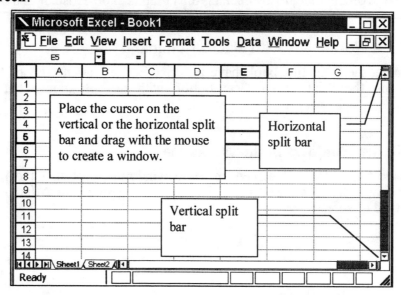

Lotus 1-2-3 Screen:

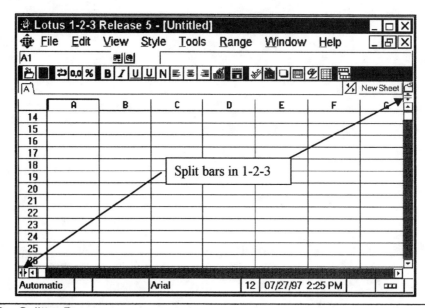

Figure 3-20:   Splitter Bars

Make sure that you have the SAMPLE template loaded. Place the mouse cursor on the horizontal splitter bar and drag it down to the middle of the screen. Then place the mouse cursor in the top window and scroll up to the beginning of the worksheet. Next, place the muse cursor in the bottom window and scroll row 25 immediately under the split window bar. The results in Excel are in the following figure.

Worksheet Screen

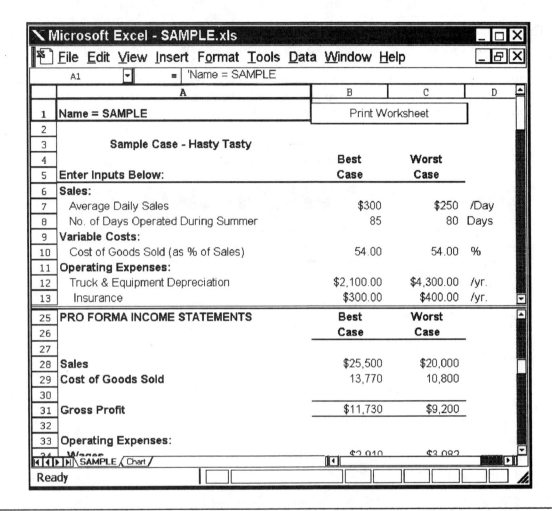

Figure 3-21: Split Worksheet into two Windows

The input values are in the top window and the pro forma income statements are in the bottom window. Use the mouse to activate a specific window. In each window press the cursor key and the cursor key a number of times. The screen will scroll down. As you scroll up you will find that the top window will not scroll past a certain point. When you reach the top of the scroll area the computer beeps. You can clear the window split by dragging the split bar back to its original position. In Microsoft Excel you can use the command WS to clear the split screens and in Lotus 1-2-3 use the command VS...

Position the report you want to see in the bottom window.. Watch the numbers in the lower window change as you make changes in the top window. This is a handy technique for seeing both inputs and results simultaneously in large worksheets.

Graphs

Most of the spreadsheet models in this book contain graphs that are already constructed for your use. These graphs are contained in individual sheets. You click on the tab labeled "CHART" to see the graph. You print the graph by clicking on the button with "Print Chart".

Some worksheets have multiple graphs, and the tabs are labeled with CHART and descriptive text.

The graphs in all worksheets are accessed at any time by clicking on the "CHART" tab. It is better to wait until you enter data into the templates before viewing the graph. Clicking the CHART tab results in the graph shown in Figure 3-22 for the Hasty Tasty case. The worksheet tabs are at the bottom of the screen in Microsoft Excel as shown in the following figure. Click on the "Sample" tab to see the worksheet, and click on the "Chart" tab to see the graph. Click on the Print Worksheet or Print Chart buttons to print.

Worksheet Screen

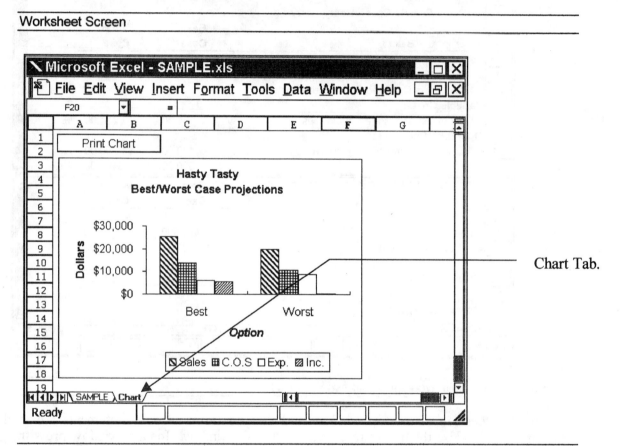

Chart Tab.

Figure 3-22:   Chart in Excel

In Lotus 1-2-3 the sheet tabs are at the top of the screen as shown in the next figure. There will be slight differences between the graphs of each package for the spreadsheets in this text, but all will have the same basic format.

Worksheet Screen
_____

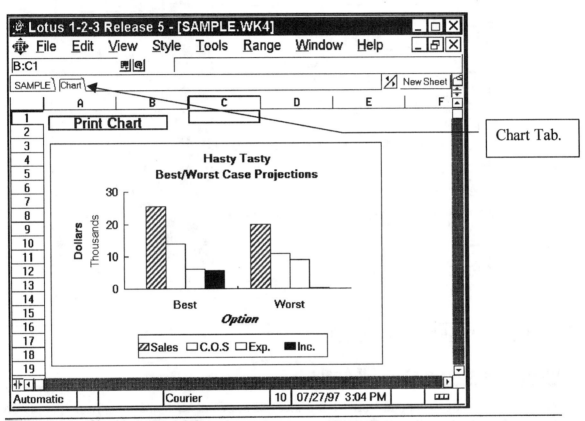

Figure 3-23:   Chart in Lotus 1-2-3

How to Change the Column Width on a Worksheet

When the number computed by an equation inside of a cell exceeds the cell's width, then the program displays "######" in Excel and "*********" in Lotus 1-2-3 instead of the number. When this event occurs you need to widen the worksheet column. You may also want to reduce the column width to see more columns at one time on the display. The procedure is the same for both Microsoft Excel and Lotus 1-2-3.

Worksheet Screen

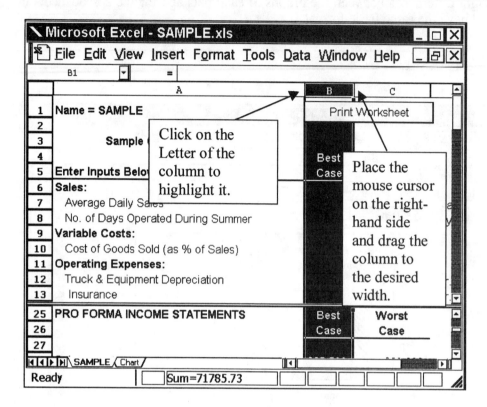

Figure 3-24: Change Column Width.

Using Goal Seek for What-If Analysis

Recent versions of Excel and Lotus 1-2-3 incorporate Goal Seek analysis. Most people doing a what-if analysis with a spreadsheet model focus on varying the key input values. For example in the Hasty Tasty case, a best case, and worst case set of inputs provide pro forma statements for each option. This type of analysis is limited to the values we set for the inputs. Goal Seek analysis allows us to reverse the process, because we specify the answer, and the program computes the required input value. For example, with Goal Seek analysis, we can compute the amount average daily sales must equal in order to generate net income equal to $7,500.

All templates in this book allow Goal Seek analysis. The following two examples illustrate it use in Excel and Lotus 1-2-3 for Windows.

Goal Seek Analysis in Excel

This example shows how to determine the average daily sales amount that will generate net income of $7,500. Make sure the Sample.XLS workbook is loaded before continuing. Access the Goal-Seek menu using the following commands.

Keystrokes for Excel	Comments
[ESC] [ESC]	If the top of the display screen shows one of the command menus, (see the introduction section of the manual) press the Escape key until the menus disappear. Skip this step if a menu is not displayed.
[ALT] TG	Access the Command menu, the Tools menu and the Goal-Seek option.
[ENTER]	Press Enter or click the left mouse button.

Table 3-10:   Goal Seek Command

Next a dialog box with the input cells shown in the next figure appears. The spreadsheet screen has been divided using the horizontal splitter bars to show both the input and output cells.

Worksheet Screen

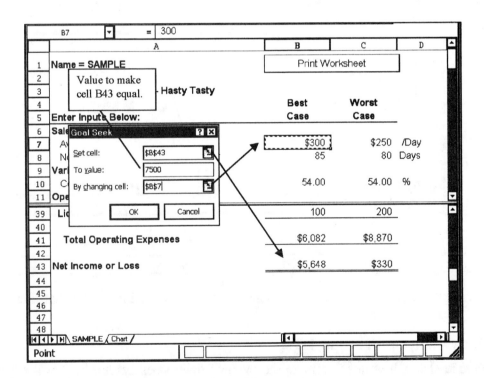

Figure 3-25:   Set Goal Seek Parameters

After setting the goal seek parameters, the program computes the answer, if it exists, that satisfies your settings. Excel shows the target value in the Goal Seek Status menu and the solution in the spreadsheet cell. For example, average daily sales of $347 generate net income of $7,500.

Worksheet Screen

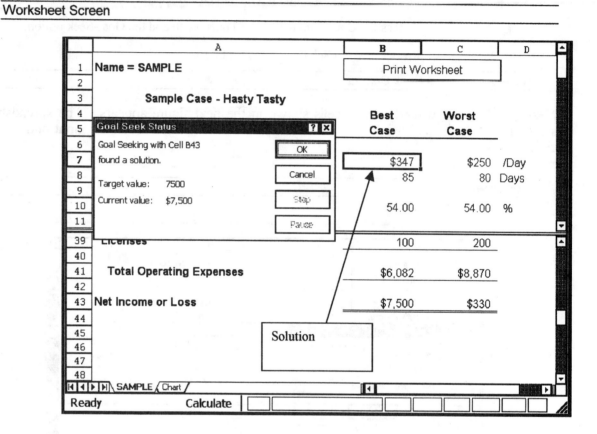

Figure 3-26   Goal Seek Status Dialog Box

You can repeat the goal seek procedure as many times as desired for your what-if analysis.

Goal Seek Analysis in Lotus 1-2-3

This example shows how to determine the average daily sales amount that will generate net income of $7,500. Make sure the Sample.WK4 workbook is loaded before continuing. Lotus 1-2-3 calls the goal seek feature the backsolver-option.

Access the Goal-Seek menu using the following commands.

Keystrokes for 1-2-3W	Comments
[ESC] [ESC]	If the top of the display screen shows one of the command menus, (see the introduction section of the manual) press the Escape key until the menus disappear. Skip this step if a menu is not displayed.
[ALT] RAB	Access the Range menu, the Analysis menu and the Backsolver-option.
[ENTER]	Press Enter or click the left mouse button.

Table 3-11:	Goal Seek Command

Next a dialog box with the input cells shown in the next figure appears. The spreadsheet screen has been divided using the horizontal splitter bars.

Worksheet Screen

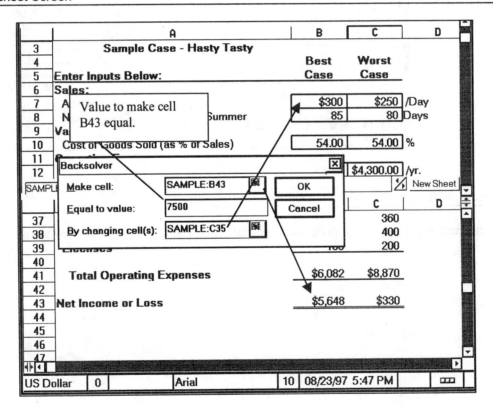

Figure 3-27:   Change Column Width.

After setting the goal seek parameters, the program computes the answer, if it exists, that satisfies your settings. Excel shows the target value in the Goal Seek Status menu and the solution in the spreadsheet cell. For example, average daily sales of $347 generate net income of $7,500.

Worksheet Screen

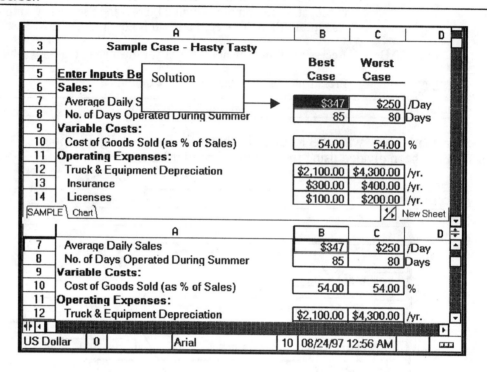

Figure 3-28: Change Column Width.

You can repeat the goal seek procedure as many times as desired for your what-if analysis

Chapter 4:
Break Even Analysis -- One Product

Introduction

This is a generalized break even analysis worksheet you can use for general case analysis. This worksheet assumes two products are produced and sold. See the worksheets named BEPONE and BEPTHREE for single and multiple product break even analysis. An overview of break even analysis is provided in Chapter 2 of Strategic Marketing Problems: Cases and Comments, 8th. ed.

This worksheet calculates the break even point in units and dollars, a contribution margin statement based on units sold, and the sales price required to earn a desired income. A graph is displayed, assuming your computer has graphic capabilities. This graph shows the total revenue, total costs, and fixed costs. You can enter the beginning unit value and the incremental units for scaling the graph.

How to Use the Worksheet

1. Fill out the input form provided for this worksheet after reading the case you are analyzing.

2. If you have not used any of the worksheets in this manual, please review the section of the manual on how to load Microsoft Excel or Lotus 1-2-3 for Windows, and the worksheets provided on the disk.

3. Load the worksheet program. After the row and column format appears, load the worksheet using the keystrokes shown in the table below. See the section of the manual on how to load worksheets if you experience difficulties.

Keystrokes for Excel or 1-2-3W	Comments
[ALT] FO	Access the Command menu, the File menu and execute the Retrieve command.
BEPONE	Either type in the file name, or highlight the name using the cursor keys, or mouse.
[ENTER]	Press the Enter key to load the worksheet.
Table 4-1: Load BEPONE worksheet	

4. After loading the worksheet, review it to make sure you know where the input cells are located. The input cells are colored differently than the rest of the cells on a color monitor. The first time you use the worksheet, most of the cells in the spreadsheet will display "NA", or "#NA", but don't worry. As you enter your input values, the NA's in the output cells will be replaced by calculated values.

Unless you have disabled the worksheet protection, only the input cells can be changed. If you accidentally attempt to change a protected (non-input) cell, the program will display an error message. Press the [ESC] key to return to normal operations.

The input sections of the worksheet for this case are boxed for emphasis in the figures below. Remember that the boxes do not show on the worksheet itself.

Worksheet

	A	B	C	D	E	F
1	Name = BEPONE					
2	Break Even Point and Profit Calculations With One Product Produced and Sold					
3	Part 1--Compute Break Even Point					
4	Enter the following:					
5	Enter Sales Price Per Unit				$16.00	
6	Enter Variable Cost Per Unit:					
7		Variable Cost #1			$5.00	
8		Variable Cost #2			$2.00	
9		Variable Cost #3			$0.00	
10		Variable Cost #4			$0.00	
11		Total Variable Cost			$7.00	
12	Enter Fixed Cost:					
13		Fixed Cost #1			$7,000	
14		Fixed Cost #2			$2,000	
15		Fixed Cost #3			$0	
16		Fixed Cost #4			$0.00	
17		Total Fixed Cost			$9,000.00	
18						
19	Break Even Points:					
20	Contribution Margin Per Unit ==>			$9.00		
21	Break Even Point in Units ==>			1,000.00		
22	Break Even Point in Dollars ==>			$16,000		
23						
24	Part 2--Compute Income Statement Based on Units Sold					
25	The selling price and costs entered above in Part 1 are used in this calculation.					
26	Enter Units Sold			1100		
27						
28	Contribution Margin Statement Based on Units Sold:					
29	Sales			$17,600		
30	Variable Costs			7,700		
31	Contribution Margin			9,900		
32	Fixed Costs			9,000		
33	Income			$900		
34						
35	Part 3--Compute Sales Price Required to Earn Desired Income:					
36	The selling price and costs entered above in Part 1 are used in this calculation.					
37						
38	Enter Desired Income in Dollars			$5,000.00		
39	Enter Units Sold			1,000		
40						
41	Calculated Sales Price Required to Earn Desired Income is:				$21.00	
42						
43	Graphing Instructions:					
44	Enter beginning unit value for graph range			0		
45	Enter incremental units for graph			100		

5.   Type into the spreadsheet your estimates of the inputs using the information from the input forms you filled out in Step 1. Use the cursor keys ⬅, ➡, ⬇, and ⬆ to move to the desired cell location. Type in the number and press either the ENTER key or one of the cursor keys. Repeat this procedure until all the necessary input cells are filled.

Viewing the Spreadsheet Schedules and Graph

You can press the cursor keys (⬅, ➡, ⬇, and ⬆), or the Page Up PG↑ and the Page Down PG↓ keys to move around the worksheet area. Press the Home key to return to the upper left-hand corner of the spreadsheet.

The worksheet contains a graph. Click on the "Chart" tab to see the graph.

Saving the Spreadsheet

After entering your estimates and examining the results, including the graph, save your spreadsheet by using the following commands.

Keystrokes for Excel or 1-2-3W	Comments
ESC ESC	If the top of the display screen shows one of the command menus, (see the introduction section of the manual) press the Escape key until the menus disappear. Skip this step if a menu is not displayed.
ALT FS	Access the Command menu, the File menu and the Save option.
ENTER	Press Enter to save under the same name. An Excel file is saved with a "XLS" suffix, and a 1-2-3 for Windows file is saved as a "WK4" file.

Table 4-2:   Save BEPONE worksheet

Printing the Worksheet

Place the mouse cursor on top of the "Print Worksheet" button to print it, and click on the "Print Chart" button to print the graph. Make sure you have a printer connected and turned on before attempting to print your results.

Bring the results of your analysis to class when the case is discussed.

Input Form for BEPONE

Name _____

Break Even Point and Profit Calculations With One Product
Produced and Sold

Part 1--Compute Break Even Point
Enter the following:
Enter Sales Price Per Unit   _____

Enter Variable Cost Per Unit and Description:

VC #1 _____   _____

VC #2 _____   _____

VC #3 _____   _____

VC #4 _____   _____

Enter Fixed Cost and Description

FC #1 _____   _____

FC #2 _____   _____

FC #3 _____   _____

FC #4 _____   _____

Part 2--Compute Income Statement Based on Units Sold
The selling price and costs entered above in Part 1
are used in this calculation.

Enter Units Sold   _____

Part 3--Compute Sales Price Required to Earn Desired Income:
The selling price and costs entered above in Part 1
are used in this calculation.

Enter Desired Income in Dollars   _____

Enter Units Sold   _____

Output Form for BEPONE

Name _____

Break Even Point and Profit Calculations With One Product
                    Produced and Sold
Part 1--Computed Break Even Point

Sales Price Per Unit   _____

Total Variable Cost Per Unit   _____

Total Fixed Cost   _____

Break Even Points:
Contribution Margin Per Unit   _____

Break Even Point in Units   _____

Break Even Point in Dollars   _____

Units Sold   _____

Part 2 -- Contribution Margin Statement Based on Units Sold

Sales   _____

Variable Costs   _____

Contribution Margin   _____

Fixed Costs   _____

Income   _____

Part 3-- Sales Price Required to Earn Desired Income:

Desired Income in Dollars   _____

        Units Sold   _____

Sales Price Required to
Earn Desired Income   _____

Chapter 5:
Break Even Analysis -- Two Products

Introduction

This is a generalized break even analysis worksheet you can use for general case analysis. This worksheet assumes two products are produced and sold. See the worksheets named BEPONE and BEPTHREE for single and multiple product break even analysis. An overview of break even analysis is provided in Chapter 2 of Strategic Marketing Problems: Cases and Comments, 8th. ed.

This worksheet calculates the break even point in units and dollars, a contribution margin statement based on units sold, and the sales price required to earn a desired income. A graph is displayed, assuming your computer has graphic capabilities. This graph shows the total revenue, total costs, and fixed costs. You can enter the beginning unit value and the incremental units for scaling the graph.

How to Use the Worksheet

1.   Fill out the input form provided for this worksheet after reading the case you are analyzing.

2.   If you have not used any of the worksheets in this manual, please review the section of the manual on how to load Microsoft Excel or Lotus 1-2-3 for Windows, and the worksheets provided on the disk.

3.   Load the worksheet program. After the row and column format appears, load the worksheet using the keystrokes shown in the table below. See the section of the manual on how to load worksheets if you experience difficulties.

Keystrokes for Excel or 1-2-3W	Comments
[ALT] FO	Access the Command menu, the File menu and execute the Retrieve command.
BEPTWO	Either type in the file name, or highlight the name using the cursor keys, or mouse.
[ENTER]	Press the Enter key to load the worksheet.

Table 5-1:   Load BEPTWO worksheet

4.   After loading the worksheet, review it to make sure you know where the input cells are located. The input cells are colored differently than the rest of the cells on a color monitor. The first time you use the worksheet, most of the cells in the spreadsheet will display "NA", or "#NA", but don't worry. As you enter your input values, the NA's in the output cells will be replaced by calculated values.

Unless you have disabled the worksheet protection, only the input cells can be changed. If you accidentally attempt to change a protected (non-input) cell, the program will display an error message. Press the [ESC] key to return to normal operations.

The input sections of the worksheet for this case are boxed for emphasis in the figures below. Remember that the boxes do not show on the worksheet itself.

Worksheet

	A	B	C	D	E	F	G
1	Name = BEPTWO						
2	Break Even Point and Profit Calculations With Two Products Produced and Sold						
3	Part 1--Compute Break Even Points						
4	Enter the following:				Product #1	Product #2	
5	Enter Sales Mix Ratio				5	3	
6	Enter Sales Price Per Unit				$15.00	$20.00	
7	Enter Variable Cost Per Unit:						
8		Variable Cost #1			$6.00	$5.00	
9		Variable Cost #2			$4.00	$6.00	
10		Variable Cost #3			$0.00	$0.00	
11		Variable Cost #4			$0.00	$0.00	
12		Total Variable Cost			$10.00	$11.00	
13	Enter Fixed Cost:						
14		Fixed Cost #1			$2,000	$4,000	
15		Fixed Cost #2			$10,000	$6,000	
16		Fixed Cost #3			$0	$0	
17		Fixed Cost #4			$0	$0	
18		Total Fixed Cost			$12,000.00	$10,000.00	
19							
20	Break Even Values						
21	Contribution Margin Per Unit				$5.00	$9.00	
22						Weighted	
23						Average Values	
24	Weighted Average Sales Price					$16.88	
25	Weighted Average Variable Cost					$10.38	
26	Weighted Average Contribution Margin					$6.50	
27							
28	Total Fixed Costs					$22,000	
29							
30	Break Even Point in Total Units Sold					3,384.62	
31	Break Even Point in Total Dollar Sales					$57,115.38	
32							
33	Units of each product that must be						
34	sold to break even:				Units	Dollars	
35	Units of Product #1				2,115.38	$31,730.77	
36	Units of Product #2				1,269.23	$25,384.62	
37		Total			3,384.62	$57,115.38	
38							
39	Part 2--Compute Income Statement Based on Units Sold.						
40	The selling prices and costs entered above in Part 1 are						
41	used in this calculation.						
42				Prod. #1	Prod. #2		
43	Enter Units Sold			2,500.00	1,300.00		
44							
45	Contribution Margin Statement Based On Units Sold:						
46				Prod. #1	Prod. #2	Total	
47	Sales			$37,500	$26,000	$63,500	
48	Variable Costs			25,000	14,300	$39,300	
49	Contribution Margin			12,500	11,700	$24,200	
50	Fixed Costs			12,000	10,000	$22,000	
51	Income			$500	$1,700	$2,200	
52							
53	Graphing Instructions:						
54	Enter beginning unit value for graph range					0	
55	Enter incremental units for graph					350	

5.   Type into the spreadsheet your estimates of the inputs using the information from the input forms you filled out in Step 1. Use the cursor keys ⬅, ➡, ⬇, and ⬆ to move to the desired cell location. Type in the number and press either the [ENTER] key or one of the cursor keys. Repeat this procedure until all the necessary input cells are filled.

Viewing the Spreadsheet Schedules and Graph

You can press the cursor keys (⬅, ➡, ⬇, and ⬆), or the Page Up [PG↑] and the Page Down [PG↓] keys to move around the worksheet area. Press the Home key to return to the upper left-hand corner of the spreadsheet.

The worksheet contains a graph. Click on the "Chart" tab to see the graph.

Saving the Spreadsheet

After entering your estimates and examining the results, including the graph, save your spreadsheet by using the following commands.

Keystrokes for Excel or 1-2-3W	Comments
[ESC] [ESC]	If the top of the display screen shows one of the command menus, (see the introduction section of the manual) press the Escape key until the menus disappear. Skip this step if a menu is not displayed.
[ALT] FS	Access the Command menu, the File menu and the Save option.
[ENTER]	Press Enter to save under the same name. An Excel file is saved with a "XLS" suffix, and a 1-2-3 for Windows file is saved as a "WK4" file.

Table 5-2:   Save BEPTWO worksheet

Printing the Worksheet

Place the mouse cursor on top of the "Print Worksheet" button to print it, and click on the "Print Chart" button to print the graph. Make sure you have a printer connected and turned on before attempting to print your results.

Bring the results of your analysis to class when the case is discussed.

Input Form for BEPTWO

Name _____

Break Even Point and Profit Calculations With Two
            Products Produced and Sold

Part 1--Compute Break Even Points

                                    Product #1 Product #2

Enter Sales Mix Ratio   _____ _____

Enter Sales Price Per Unit   _____ _____

Enter Variable Cost Per
Unit and Description:
VC # 1   _____ _____

VC # 2   _____ _____

VC # 3   _____ _____

VC # 4   _____ _____

Enter Fixed Costs and Description:
FC # 1   _____ _____

FC # 2   _____ _____

FC # 3   _____ _____

FC # 4   _____ _____

Part 2--Compute Income Statement Based on Units Sold.
The selling prices and costs entered above in Part 1 are
used in this calculation.
                                    Prod. #1   Prod. #2

Enter Units Sold   _____ _____

Output Form for BEPTWO - Page 1 of 2

Name _____

Break Even Point and Profit Calculations With Two
        Products Produced and Sold

Part 1--Break Even Points

	Product #1	Product #2
Sales Mix Ratio	_____	_____
Sales Price Per Unit	_____	_____
Total Variable Cost	_____	_____
Total Fixed Cost	_____	_____
Contribution Margin Per Unit	_____	_____

	Weighted Average Values
Weighted Average Sales Price	_____
Weighted Average Variable Cost	_____
Weighted Average Contribution Margin	_____
Total Fixed Costs	_____
Break Even Point in Total Units Sold	_____
Break Even Point in Total Dollar Sales	_____

Units of each product that must be sold to
break even:

	Units	Dollars
Units of Product #1	_____	_____
Units of Product #2	_____	_____
Total	_____	_____

Output Form for BEPTWO - Page 2 of 2

Part 2--Compute Income Statement Based on Units Sold.
The selling prices and costs entered above in Part 1 are
used in this calculation.

	Prod. #1	Prod. #2
Units Sold	_____	_____

Contribution Margin Statement Based On Units Sold:

	Prod. #1	Prod. #2	Total
Sales	_____	_____	_____
Variable Costs	_____	_____	_____
Contribution Margin	_____	_____	_____
Fixed Costs	_____	_____	_____
Income	_____	_____	_____

Chapter 6:
Break Even Analysis -- Three Products

Introduction

This is a generalized break even analysis worksheet you can use for general case analysis. This worksheet assumes three products are produced and sold. See the worksheets named BEPONE and BEPTWO for a one and two product break even analysis. An overview of break even analysis is provided in Chapter 2 of Strategic Marketing Problems: Cases and Comments, 8th. ed.

This worksheet calculates the break even point in units and dollars, a contribution margin statement based on units sold, and the sales price required to earn a desired income. A graph is displayed, assuming your computer has graphic capabilities. This graph shows the total revenue, total costs, and fixed costs. You can enter the beginning unit value and the incremental units for scaling the graph.

How to Use the Worksheet

1.   Fill out the input form provided for this worksheet after reading the case you are analyzing.

2.   If you have not used any of the worksheets in this manual, please review the section of the manual on how to load Microsoft Excel or Lotus 1-2-3 for Windows, and the worksheets provided on the disk.

3.   Load the worksheet program. After the row and column format appears, load the worksheet using the keystrokes shown in the table below. See the section of the manual on how to load worksheets if you experience difficulties.

Keystrokes for Excel or 1-2-3W	Comments
[ALT] FO	Access the Command menu, the File menu and execute the Retrieve command.
BEPTHREE	Either type in the file name, or highlight the name using the cursor keys, or mouse.
[ENTER]	Press the Enter key to load the worksheet.
Table 6-1: Load BEPTHREE worksheet	

4.   After loading the worksheet, review it to make sure you know where the input cells are located. The input cells are colored differently than the rest of the cells on a color monitor. The first time you use the worksheet, most of the cells in the spreadsheet will display "NA", or "#NA", but don't worry. As you enter your input values, the NA's in the output cells will be replaced by calculated values.

Unless you have disabled the worksheet protection, only the input cells can be changed. If you accidentally attempt to change a protected (non-input) cell, the program will display an error message. Press the [ESC] key to return to normal operations.

The input sections of the worksheet for this case are boxed for emphasis in the figures below. Remember that the boxes do not show on the worksheet itself.

Worksheet

	A	B	C	D	E	F	G
1	Name = BEPTHREE						
2							
3		**Break Even Point and Profit Calculations With Three**					
4		**Products Produced and Sold.**					
5							
6	**Part 1--Compute Break Even Points**						
7	Enter the following:				**Product #1**	**Product #2**	**Product #3**
8	Enter Sales Mix Ratio				5	3	2
9	Enter Sales Price Per Unit				$18.00	$20.00	$35.00
10	Enter Variable Cost Per Unit:						
11	Variable Cost #1				$6.00	$7.00	$9.00
12	Variable Cost #2				$4.00	$4.00	$4.00
13	Variable Cost #3				$0.00	$0.00	$0.00
14	Variable Cost #4				$0.00	$0.00	$0.00
15							
16	Total Variable Cost per Unit				$10.00	$11.00	$13.00
17	Enter Fixed Cost:						
18	Fixed Cost #1				$3,000	$3,200	$3,500
19	Fixed Cost #2				$2,000	$2,100	$1,000
20	Fixed Cost #3				$0	$0	$0
21	Fixed Cost #4				$0.00	$0.00	$0.00
22	Total Fixed Cost				$5,000.00	$5,300.00	$4,500.00
23							
24	**Break Even Values:**						
25	Contribution Margin Per Unit ==>				$8.00	$9.00	$22.00
26							
27						**Weighted**	
28						**Average Values**	
29	Weighted Average Sales Price ==>					$22.00	
30	Weighted Average Variable Cost ==>					$10.90	
31	Weighted Average Contribution Margin ==>					$11.10	
32							
33	Total Fixed Costs					$14,800.00	
34							
35	Break Even Point in Total Units Sold ==>					1,333.33 Units	
36	Break Even Point in Total Dollar Sales ==>					$29,333.33 Sales Dollars	
37							
38	Units of each product that must be sold to						
39	break even:				**Units**	**Dollars**	
40	Units of Product #1				666.67	$12,000.00	
41	Units of Product #2				400.00	$8,000.00	
42	Units of Product #3				266.67	$9,333.33	
43	Total				1,333	$29,333.33	
44							
45	**Part 2--Compute Income Statement Based on Units Sold**						
46	The selling prices and costs entered above in Part 1 are						
47	used in this calculation.						
48				**Product #1**	**Product #2**	**Product #3**	
49	Enter Units Sold			1,214.01	728.40	242.80	
50							
51	**Contribution Margin Statement Based On Units Sold:**						
52				**Product #1**	**Product #2**	**Product #3**	**Total**
53	Sales			$21,852	$14,568	$8,498	$44,918
54	Variable Costs			12,140	8,012	3,156	$23,309
55	Contribution Margin			9,712	6,556	5,342	$21,609
56	Fixed Costs			5,000	5,300	4,500	14,800
57	Income			$4,712	$1,256	$842	$6,809
58							
59							

5.   Type into the spreadsheet your estimates of the inputs using the information from the input forms you filled out in Step 1. Use the cursor keys ⬅, ➡, ⬇, and ⬆ to move to the desired cell location. Type in the number and press either the ⏎ key or one of the cursor keys. Repeat this procedure until all the necessary input cells are filled.

Viewing the Spreadsheet Schedules and Graph

You can press the cursor keys (⬅, ➡, ⬇, and ⬆), or the Page Up ⤒ and the Page Down ⤓ keys to move around the worksheet area. Press the Home key to return to the upper left-hand corner of the spreadsheet.

The worksheet contains a graph. Click on the "Chart" tab to see the graph.

Saving the Spreadsheet

After entering your estimates and examining the results, including the graph, save your spreadsheet by using the following commands.

Keystrokes for Excel or 1-2-3W	Comments
ESC ESC	If the top of the display screen shows one of the command menus, (see the introduction section of the manual) press the Escape key until the menus disappear. Skip this step if a menu is not displayed.
ALT FS	Access the Command menu, the File menu and the Save option.
ENTER	Press Enter to save under the same name. An Excel file is saved with a "XLS" suffix, and a 1-2-3 for Windows file is saved as a "WK4" file.

Table 6-2:   Save BEPTHREE worksheet

Printing the Worksheet

Place the mouse cursor on top of the "Print Worksheet" button to print it, and click on the "Print Chart" button to print the graph. Make sure you have a printer connected and turned on before attempting to print your results.

Bring the results of your analysis to class when the case is discussed.

Input Form for BEPTHREE

Name _____

Break Even Point and Profit Calculations With Three
Products Produced and Sold.

Part 1--Compute Break Even Points
Enter the following: Product #1 Product #2 Product #3

Enter Sales Mix Ratio   _____ _____ _____

Enter Sales Price Per Unit   _____ _____ _____

Enter Variable Cost Per Unit
and Description:
VC # 1   _____ _____ _____

VC # 2   _____ _____ _____

VC # 3   _____ _____ _____

VC # 4   _____ _____ _____

Enter Fixed Cost and Description:
FC # 1   _____ _____ _____

FC # 2   _____ _____ _____

FC # 3   _____ _____ _____

FC # 4   _____ _____ _____

Part 2--Compute Income Statement Based on Units Sold
The selling prices and costs entered above in Part 1. are
used in this calculation.

                               Prod. #1   Prod. #2   Prod. #3

Enter Units Sold   _____ _____ _____

Output Form for BEPTHREE - Page 1 of 2

Name _____

Break Even Point and Profit Calculations With Three
Products Produced and Sold.

Part 1--Compute Break Even Points

	Product #1	Product #2	Product #3
Sales Mix Ratio	_____	_____	_____
Sales Price Per Unit	_____	_____	_____
Total Variable Cost	_____	_____	_____
Total Fixed Cost	_____	_____	_____
Contribution Margin Per Unit	_____	_____	_____

Weighted Average Values

Weighted Average Sales Price _____

Weighted Average Variable Cost _____

Weighted Average Contribution Margin _____

Total Fixed Costs _____

Break Even Values:
Break Even Point in Total Units Sold _____

Break Even Point in Total Dollar Sales _____

Units of each product that must be sold to
break even:

	Units	Dollars
Units of Product #1	_____	_____
Units of Product #2	_____	_____
Units of Product #3	_____	_____
Total	_____	_____

Output Form for BEPTHREE - Page 2 of 2

Part 2--Compute Income Statement Based on Units Sold
the selling prices and costs entered above in Part 1 are
used in this calculation.

	Prod. #1	Prod. #2	Prod. #3
Enter Units Sold	_____	_____	_____

Contribution Margin Statement Based On Units Sold:

	Prod. #1	Prod. #2	Prod. #3	Total
Sales	_____	_____	_____	_____
Variable Costs	_____	_____	_____	_____
Contribution Margin	_____	_____	_____	_____
Fixed Costs	_____	_____	_____	_____
Income	_____	_____	_____	_____

Chapter 7:

Cannibalization Assessment

Introduction

This is a generalized worksheet for cannibalization assessment that you can use for general case analysis. An overview of cannibalization assessment is provided in Chapter 2 of Strategic Marketing Problems: Cases and Comments, 8th. ed., pp. 40-43.

Please refer to the text for a discussion of cannibalization assessment.

How to Use the Worksheet

1. Fill out the input form provided for this worksheet after reading the case you are analyzing.

2. If you have not used any of the worksheets in this manual, please review the section of the manual on how to load Microsoft Excel or Lotus 1-2-3 for Windows, and the worksheets provided on the disk.

3. Load the worksheet program. After the row and column format appears, load the worksheet using the keystrokes shown in the table below. See the section of the manual on how to load worksheets if you experience difficulties.

Keystrokes for Excel or 1-2-3W	Comments
[ALT] FO	Access the Command menu, the File menu and execute the Retrieve command.
CANNIBAL	Either type in the file name, or highlight the name using the cursor keys, or mouse.
[ENTER]	Press the Enter key to load the worksheet.
Table 7-1: Load CANNIBAL worksheet	

4. After loading the worksheet, review it to make sure you know where the input cells are located. The input cells are colored differently than the rest of the cells on a color monitor. The first time you use the worksheet, most of the cells in the spreadsheet will display "NA", or "#NA", but don't worry. As you enter your input values, the NA's in the output cells will be replaced by calculated values.

Unless you have disabled the worksheet protection, only the input cells can be changed. If you accidentally attempt to change a protected (non-input) cell, the program will display an error message. Press the [ESC] key to return to normal operations.

The input sections of the worksheet for this case are boxed for emphasis in the figures below. Remember that the boxes do not show on the worksheet itself.

Worksheet

	A	B	C	D	E	F	G
1	Name = Cannibal						
2			Cannibalization Assessment				
3	Inputs:						
4	Existing product volume in units.					1,000,000	
5	Percent of existing products volume that is						
6	cannibalized by new product.					50	
7	Incremental (new) volume for new						
8	product in units.					500,000	
9	Selling price per unit for existing product					$1.00	
10	Variable cost per unit for existing product					$0.20	
11	Selling price per unit for new product					$1.10	
12	Variable cost per unit for new product					$0.40	
13							
14	Analysis:						
15						Contribution Margin	
16					Unit Volume	Per Unit	Dollars
17	Existing product sales				500,000	$0.80	$400,000
18	New product sales:						
19	Cannibalized Volume				500,000	$0.70	$350,000
20	Incremental Volume				500,000	$0.70	$350,000
21	Total				1,500,000		$1,100,000
22	Original forecast volume for existing product				1,000,000	$0.80	$800,000
23	Increase (decrease) in unit sales and contribution						
24	margin due to cannibalization				500,000		$300,000

5.   Type into the spreadsheet your estimates of the inputs using the information from the input forms you filled out in Step 1. Use the cursor keys ⬅, ➡, ⬇, and ⬆ to move to the desired cell location. Type in the number and press either the [ENTER] key or one of the cursor keys. Repeat this procedure until all the necessary input cells are filled.

Viewing the Spreadsheet Schedules

You can press the cursor keys (⬅, ➡, ⬇, and ⬆), or the Page Up [PG↑] and the Page Down [PG↓] keys to move around the worksheet area. Press the Home key to return to the upper left-hand corner of the spreadsheet.

The worksheet does not contains a graph.

Saving the Spreadsheet

After entering your estimates and examining the results, including the graph, save your spreadsheet by using the following commands.

Keystrokes for Excel or 1-2-3W	Comments
[ESC] [ESC]	If the top of the display screen shows one of the command menus, (see the introduction section of the manual) press the Escape key until the menus disappear. Skip this step if a menu is not displayed.
[ALT] FS	Access the Command menu, the File menu and the Save option.
[ENTER]	Press Enter to save under the same name. An Excel file is saved with a "XLS" suffix, and a 1-2-3 for Windows file is saved as a "WK4" file.

Table 7-2:   Save CANNIBAL worksheet

Printing the Worksheet

Place the mouse cursor on top of the "Print Worksheet" button to print it, and click on the "Print Chart" button to print the graph. Make sure you have a printer connected and turned on before attempting to print your results.

Bring the results of your analysis to class when the case is discussed.

Input Form for CANNIBAL

Name _____

Cannibalization Assessment

Existing product volume in units.   _____

Percent of existing products volume
  that is cannibalized by new product.   _____

Incremental (new) volume for new
  product in units.   _____

Selling price per unit for existing product   _____

Variable cost per unit for existing product   _____

Selling price per unit for new product   _____

Variable cost per unit for new product   _____

Output Form for CANNIBAL

Name _____

	Unit Volume	Contribution Margin Per Unit	Dollars
Existing product sales	_____	_____	_____
New product sales:			
Cannibalized Volume	_____	_____	_____
Incremental Volume	_____	_____	_____
Total	_____		_____
Original forecast volume for existing product	_____	_____	_____
Increase (decrease) in unit sales and contribution margin due to cannibalization	_____		_____

Chapter 8:
Sales Forecast -- Units

Introduction

This is a generalized worksheet for forecasting sales based on units sold. This analysis assumes you have the sales prices in terms of units. The variable costs can be expressed as a percent of sales, or as a dollar amount per unit

How to Use the Worksheet

1. Fill out the input form provided for this worksheet after reading the case you are analyzing.

2. If you have not used any of the worksheets in this manual, please review the section of the manual on how to load Microsoft Excel or Lotus 1-2-3 for Windows, and the worksheets provided on the disk.

3. Load the worksheet program. After the row and column format appears, load the worksheet using the keystrokes shown in the table below. See the section of the manual on how to load worksheets if you experience difficulties.

Keystrokes for Excel or 1-2-3W	Comments
[ALT] FO	Access the Command menu, the File menu and execute the Retrieve command.
FCASTUNT	Either type in the file name, or highlight the name using the cursor keys, or mouse.
[ENTER]	Press the Enter key to load the worksheet.

Table 8-1: Load FCASTUNT worksheet

4. After loading the worksheet, review it to make sure you know where the input cells are located. The input cells are colored differently than the rest of the cells on a color monitor. The first time you use the worksheet, most of the cells in the spreadsheet will display "NA", or "#NA", but don't worry. As you enter your input values, the NA's in the output cells will be replaced by calculated values.

Unless you have disabled the worksheet protection, only the input cells can be changed. If you accidentally attempt to change a protected (non-input) cell, the program will display an error message. Press the [ESC] key to return to normal operations.

The input sections of the worksheet for this case are boxed for emphasis in the figures below. Remember that the boxes do not show on the worksheet itself.

Worksheet

	A	B	C	D	E	F	G
1	Name = FCASTUNT						
2	This model generates a sales forcast based on your estimates of						
3	units sold and other unit values.						
4	Any cell that is unprotected can be changed. As a result, changing the						
5	labels in the input cells changes them in the income statements. Any						
6	labels changed will be reflected in the statements.						
7							
8	Sales Forecast Model Based on Units Sold:						
9	Inputs:						
10	Company Name				Brand Z Company		
11							
12	Product Title				Product 1	Product 2	Product 3
13	Units Sold				1000	1100	1200
14	Sales Price Per Unit				$75.00	$80.00	$90.00
15	Sales Discounts and						
16	Allowances as Percent of Sales				2	3	3
17	*Type in your own descriptions of the variable costs.*						
18	Enter Variable Costs per unit sold:						
19	Variable Cost #1 Per Unit				$12.00	$11.00	$12.00
20	Variable Cost #2 Per Unit				$13.00	$15.00	$13.00
21	Variable Cost #3 Per Unit				#N/A	#N/A	#N/A
22							
23	Enter Variable Costs expressed as a						
24	percent of net sales:						
25	Variable Cost #4 as percent of sales				4.00	4.00	4.00
26	Variable Cost #5 as percent of sales				7.00	7.00	7.00
27	Variable Cost #6 as percent of sales				#N/A	#N/A	#N/A
28	Variable Cost #7 as percent of sales				#N/A	#N/A	#N/A
29							
30	Type in your own descriptions of						
31	the fixed costs.						
32	Fixed Cost #1				$3,000	$3,000	$3,000
33	Fixed Cost #2				$2,000	$2,000	$2,000
34	Fixed Cost #3				#N/A	#N/A	#N/A
35	Fixed Cost #4				#N/A	#N/A	#N/A
36	Fixed Cost #5				#N/A	#N/A	#N/A
37							

5.   Type into the spreadsheet your estimates of the inputs using the information from the input forms you filled out in Step 1. Use the cursor keys ⬅, ➡, ⬇, and ⬆ to move to the desired cell location. Type in the number and press either the ⏎ENTER key or one of the cursor keys. Repeat this procedure until all the necessary input cells are filled.

Viewing the Spreadsheet Schedules and Graph

You can press the cursor keys (⬅, ➡, ⬇, and ⬆), or the Page Up [PG↑] and the Page Down [PG↓] keys to move around the worksheet area. Press the Home key to return to the upper left-hand corner of the spreadsheet.

The worksheet contains a graph. Click on the "Chart" tab to see the graph.

Saving the Spreadsheet

After entering your cstimates and examining the results, including the graph, save your spreadsheet by using the following commands.

Keystrokes for Excel or 1-2-3W	Comments
[ESC] [ESC]	If the top of the display screen shows one of the command menus, (see the introduction section of the manual) press the Escape key until the menus disappear. Skip this step if a menu is not displayed.
[ALT] FS	Access the Command menu, the File menu and the Save option.
[ENTER]	Press Enter to save under the same name. An Excel file is saved with a "XLS" suffix, and a 1-2-3 for Windows file is saved as a "WK4" file.

Table 8-2:   Save FCASTUNT worksheet

Printing the Worksheet

Place the mouse cursor on top of the "Print Worksheet" button to print it, and click on the "Print Chart" button to print the graph. Make sure you have a printer connected and turned on before attempting to print your results.

Bring the results of your analysis to class when the case is discussed.

Input Form for FCASTUNT

Name _____

Sales Forecast Model Based on Units Sold

Inputs:Company Name   _____

	Product 1	Product 2	Product 3
Units Sold	_____	_____	_____
Sales Price Per Unit	_____	_____	_____
Sales Discounts and Allowances as Percent of Sales	_____	_____	_____

Type in your own descriptions of
the variable costs.
Variable Costs per unit sold:

VC #1/Unit _____	_____	_____	_____
VC #2/Unit _____	_____	_____	_____
VC #3/Unit _____	_____	_____	_____

Variable Costs expressed as a
 percent of net sales:

VC #4 as % _____	_____	_____	_____
VC #5 as % _____	_____	_____	_____
VC #6 as % _____	_____	_____	_____
VC #7 as % _____	_____	_____	_____

Type in your own descriptions of
the fixed costs.

FC #1 _____	_____	_____	_____
FC #2 _____	_____	_____	_____
FC #3 _____	_____	_____	_____
FC #4 _____	_____	_____	_____
FC #5 _____	_____	_____	_____

Output Form for FCASTUNT

Name _____
Company Name
                                    _____
                                         Income Statement

                                    Product 1   Product 2   Product 3
                                    _____   _____   _____

Sales   _____   _____   _____

  Sales Discounts & Allowances   _____   _____   _____

Net Sales   _____   _____   _____

Variable Costs,
Amount and Description:
VC #1 _____   _____   _____   _____

VC #2 _____   _____   _____   _____

VC #3 _____   _____   _____   _____

VC #4 _____   _____   _____   _____

VC #5 _____   _____   _____   _____

VC #6 _____   _____   _____   _____

VC #7 _____   _____   _____   _____

Total Variable Costs   _____   _____   _____

Contribution Margin   _____   _____   _____

Fixed Costs :
Amount and Description:
FC #1 _____   _____   _____   _____

FC #2 _____   _____   _____   _____

FC #3 _____   _____   _____   _____

FC #4 _____   _____   _____   _____

FC #5 _____   _____   _____   _____

Total Fixed Costs   _____   _____   _____

Profit   _____   _____   _____

Chapter 9:
Sales Forecast - Dollars

Introduction

This is a generalized worksheet for forecasting sales based on sales dollars. This analysis assumes you have the total sales by product in dollars. The variable costs are expressed as a percent of sales

How to Use the Worksheet

1.   Fill out the input form provided for this worksheet after reading the case you are analyzing.

2.   If you have not used any of the worksheets in this manual, please review the section of the manual on how to load Microsoft Excel or Lotus 1-2-3 for Windows, and the worksheets provided on the disk.

3.   Load the worksheet program. After the row and column format appears, load the worksheet using the keystrokes shown in the table below. See the section of the manual on how to load worksheets if you experience difficulties.

Keystrokes for Excel or 1-2-3W	Comments
[ALT] FO	Access the Command menu, the File menu and execute the Retrieve command.
FCASTDOL	Either type in the file name, or highlight the name using the cursor keys, or mouse.
[ENTER]	Press the Enter key to load the worksheet.

Table 9-1:   Load FCASTDOL worksheet

4.   After loading the worksheet, review it to make sure you know where the input cells are located. The input cells are colored differently than the rest of the cells on a color monitor. The first time you use the worksheet, most of the cells in the spreadsheet will display "NA", or "#NA", but don't worry. As you enter your input values, the NA's in the output cells will be replaced by calculated values.

Unless you have disabled the worksheet protection, only the input cells can be changed. If you accidentally attempt to change a protected (non-input) cell, the program will display an error message. Press the [ESC] key to return to normal operations.

The input sections of the worksheet for this case are boxed for emphasis in the figures below. Remember that the boxes do not show on the worksheet itself.

Worksheet

	A	B	C	D	E	F	G
1	Name = FCASTDOL						
2	Any cell that is unprotected can be changed. As a result, changing the						
3	labels in the input cells changes them in the income statements. Any						
4	labels changed will be reflected in the statements.						
5							
6	Sales Forecast Model Based on Dollar Sales:						
7	Inputs:						
8	Company Name				Brand Q Ltd.		
9							
10	Product Title				Product 1	Product 2	Product 3
11	Total Sales in Dollars				$100,000	$100,000	$100,000
12	Sales Discounts and						
13	Allowances as Percent of Sales				2	2.5	3
14	Cost of Goods Sold as						
15	Percent of Sales				60.00	65.00	77.00
16							
17	*Type in your own descriptions of*						
18	*the Selling and Administrative costs.*						
19	Variable Costs Sell. & Adm.						
20	Expenses expressed as a percent						
21	of net sales:						
22	Variable Cost #1 as percent of sales				4.00	4.00	4.00
23	Variable Cost #2 as percent of sales				7.00	7.00	7.00
24	Variable Cost #3 as percent of sales				1.00	1.00	1.00
25	Variable Cost #4 as percent of sales				#N/A	#N/A	#N/A
26	Variable Cost #5 as percent of sales				#N/A	#N/A	#N/A
27	Variable Cost #6 as percent of sales				#N/A	#N/A	#N/A
28							
29	Type in your own descriptions of						
30	the fixed costs.						
31	Fixed Cost #1				$3,000	$3,000	$3,000
32	Fixed Cost #2				$2,000	$2,000	$2,000
33	Fixed Cost #3				#N/A	#N/A	#N/A
34	Fixed Cost #4				#N/A	#N/A	#N/A
35	Fixed Cost #5				#N/A	#N/A	#N/A
36							

5.   Type into the spreadsheet your estimates of the inputs using the information from the input forms you filled out in Step 1. Use the cursor keys ⬅, ➡, ⬇, and ⬆ to move to the desired cell location. Type in the number and press either the ENTER key or one of the cursor keys. Repeat this procedure until all the necessary input cells are filled.

Viewing the Spreadsheet Schedules and Graph

You can press the cursor keys ([←], [→], [↓], and [↑]), or the Page Up [PG↑] and the Page Down [PG↓] keys to move around the worksheet area. Press the Home key to return to the upper left-hand corner of the spreadsheet.

The worksheet contains a graph. Click on the "Chart" tab to see the graph.

Saving the Spreadsheet

After entering your estimates and examining the results, including the graph, save your spreadsheet by using the following commands.

Keystrokes for Excel or 1-2-3W	Comments
[ESC] [ESC]	If the top of the display screen shows one of the command menus, (see the introduction section of the manual) press the Escape key until the menus disappear. Skip this step if a menu is not displayed.
[ALT] FS	Access the Command menu, the File menu and the Save option.
[ENTER]	Press Enter to save under the same name. An Excel file is saved with a "XLS" suffix, and a 1-2-3 for Windows file is saved as a "WK4" file.

Table 9-2:   Save FCASTDOL worksheet

Printing the Worksheet

Place the mouse cursor on top of the "Print Worksheet" button to print it, and click on the "Print Chart" button to print the graph. Make sure you have a printer connected and turned on before attempting to print your results.

Bring the results of your analysis to class when the case is discussed.

Input Form for FCASTDOL

Name _____

Sales Forecast Model Based on Dollar Sales

Inputs:

Company Name _____

	Product 1	Product 2	Product 3
Total Sales	_____	_____	_____
Sales Discounts and Allowances as Percent of Sales	_____	_____	_____
Cost of Goods Sold as Percent of Sales	_____	_____	_____

Type in your own descriptions of
the Selling and Administrative costs.

Variable Costs Sell. & Adm.
 Expenses expressed as a percent
 of net sales:

VC #1 % _____ _____ _____ _____

VC #2 % _____ _____ _____ _____

VC #3 % _____ _____ _____ _____

VC #4 % _____ _____ _____ _____

VC #5 % _____ _____ _____ _____

VC #6 % _____ _____ _____ _____

Type in your own descriptions of
the fixed costs.

FC #1 _____ _____ _____ _____

FC #2 _____ _____ _____ _____

FC #3 _____ _____ _____ _____

FC #4 _____ _____ _____ _____

FC #5 _____ _____ _____ _____

Output Form for FCASTDOL

Name _____

Company Name

	Income Statement		
	Product 1	Product 2	Product 3
Sales	_____	_____	_____
Sales Discounts & Allowances	_____	_____	_____
Net Sales	_____	_____	_____
Cost of Goods Sold	_____	_____	_____
Gross Margin	_____	_____	_____

Selling and Administrative Costs:

	Product 1	Product 2	Product 3
VC #1 %	_____	_____	_____
VC #2 %	_____	_____	_____
VC #3 %	_____	_____	_____
VC #4 %	_____	_____	_____
VC #5 %	_____	_____	_____
VC #6 %	_____	_____	_____
FC #1	_____	_____	_____
FC #2	_____	_____	_____
FC #3	_____	_____	_____
FC #4	_____	_____	_____
FC #5	_____	_____	_____
Total Selling and Admin. Costs	_____	_____	_____
Profit	_____	_____	_____

Chapter 10:
Regression Analysis

Introduction

This is a generalized worksheet for computing a linear regression analysis and graph with one independent and one dependent variable. You can add or delete rows using macros. Special macros for inserting and deleting rows enable an analysis with as few as five or as many as 100 or more data points.

The worksheet fits the data to a linear equation in the form: $y' = a + b*x$.

The program computes:

y' The projected value based on an X value and the computed intercept and slope.

Intercept (a)   The intercept on the y-axis for the linear equation.

Slope (b)   The amount the of the change in y when x changes one unit.

r The correlation coefficient measures the strength of the linear relationship, and it varies between minus one and plus one. A value close to either minus one or plus one indicates high correlation.

r^2 The index of determination, which measures the goodness of the fit of the projected line. This value varies between zero and one, with a value close to one indicating a good data fit, and a value close to zero indicating no fit or a poor data fit.

S_e The standard error of residuals. About 95 percent of the time the actual results of the equation will be within plus or minus two standard errors of the regression line.

S_b The standard error of the slope. About 95 percent of the time the actual slope will be within plus or minus two standard errors of the slope.

T-value   The slope divided by S_b. If this value is two or three, then the slope is probably not zero.

Refer to a statistics text for more details. The equations are documented in the spreadsheet.

The data in the worksheet currently computes a linear regression with the number of distribution outlets as the independent variable (x) and the Sales as the dependent variable (y). The resulting equation is $y' = \$74.5733 + \$6.3556\,x$. This equation says that each additional distribution outlet will generate $74.5733 (millions) in sales. The correlation index (r) is 80.20% which means there is strong linear relationship and the variables are correlated. The index of determination (r^2) is 64.32%, which means that about two-thirds of the variation between the data points and the y mean is explained by the equation. The T-value is 4.2454 and means the slope is probably not zero. If you project the sales with 30 stores, the estimated total sales will be $265.24. About 95 percent of the time, the actual sales will be within plus or minus two standard errors of the residuals, $50.07 or $265.24 +/- $100.14.

How to Use the Worksheet

1.   Fill out the input form provided for this worksheet after reading the case you are analyzing.

2.   If you have not used any of the worksheets in this manual, please review the section of the manual on how to load Microsoft Excel or Lotus 1-2-3 for Windows, and the worksheets provided on the disk.

3.   Load the worksheet program. After the row and column format appears, load the worksheet using the keystrokes shown in the table below. See the section of the manual on how to load worksheets if you experience difficulties.

Keystrokes for Excel or 1-2-3W	Comments
[ALT] FO	Access the Command menu, the File menu and execute the Retrieve command.
REGRESS	Either type in the file name, or highlight the name using the cursor keys, or mouse.
[ENTER]	Press the Enter key to load the worksheet.

Table 10-1:   Load REGRESS worksheet

4.   After loading the worksheet, review it to make sure you know where the input cells are located. The input cells are colored differently than the rest of the cells on a color monitor. The first time you use the worksheet, most of the cells in the spreadsheet will display "NA", or "#NA", but don't worry. As you enter your input values, the NA's in the output cells will be replaced by calculated values.

You will probably need to add or delete rows so the number of observations in the template fit your exercise. Click on the Insert Row button to add a row and on the Delete Row button to delete a row. The macro removes and replaces rows from the middle of the data. You should always have at least five observations when using this template. The upper limit on the number of observations is the size of the memory in your computer and the program limits.

Unless you have disabled the worksheet protection, only the input cells can be changed. If you accidentally attempt to change a protected (non-input) cell, the program will display an error message. Press the [ESC] key to return to normal operations.

The input sections of the worksheet for this case are boxed for emphasis in the figure below. Remember that the boxes do not show on the worksheet.

Worksheet

	A	B	C	D	E	F	G
1	**Name = REGRESS**						
2	NOTE:		You can add and delete rows at the Insert Point to this				
3			spreadsheet, but a minimum of five is necessary.				
4							
5	INSERT		Press Button add one row to regression			Insert Row	
6							
7	DELETE		Press Button to add one row in regression			Delete Row	
8	**Inputs:**						
9	Enter the first line of the title for your graph below:						
10	Title 1 =>		Distribution Outlets to Total Sales				
11	Enter the second line of title for your graph below:						
12	Title 2 =>		in 12 Sales Regions				
13	Enter the title for the x-axis below						
14	X Axis Title		Distribution Outlets				
15	Enter the title for the y-axis below.						
16	Y Axis Title		Sales (in millions)				
17							
18	**Enter data points in the unprotected cells below.**						
19		Observation					
20		Number	X	Y	Y'	+2 STD	-2 STD
21	Data Points	1	33.00	345.00	283.26	406.77	159.75
22		2	46.00	350.00	352.74	476.25	229.23
23		3	29.00	275.00	261.88	385.39	138.37
24		4	33.00	295.00	283.26	406.77	159.75
25		5	44.00	225.00	342.05	465.56	218.54
26		6	50.00	425.00	374.11	497.62	250.60
27		7	50.00	425.00	374.11	497.62	250.60
28		8	20.00	183.00	213.78	337.29	90.27
29		9	39.00	374.00	315.32	438.83	191.81
30		10	45.00	278.00	347.39	470.90	223.88
31		11	33.00	217.00	283.26	406.77	159.75
32		12	26.00	285.00	245.85	369.36	122.34
33	No. Data Points	12					
34	Totals		448	3,677	3,677		
35	Average		37.33	306.42			
36	**Results:**						
37	Intercept (a) =		106.8894				
38	Slope (b) =		5.3445		This equation says that		
39	Equation =		Y = 106.89 + 5.34*X		each time you increase		
40	Correlation Coefficient (R)		66.47%		Distribution Outlets by one,		
41	Index of Determination (R^2)		44.18%		Sales (in millions)		
42	Standard Error of Residuals (Se) =		61.7550		will change by 5.34 .		
43	Standard Error of						
44	Coefficient (Slope) (Sb) =		1.8998				
45	T-Value =		2.8132				
46							
47	**What-If Analysis:**						
48	Enter X value.		30				
49	Projected Y value.		267.22 +/- 2 STD = 123.51				
50							

5.   Type into the spreadsheet your estimates of the inputs using the information from the input forms you filled out in Step 1. Use the cursor keys ⬅, ➡, ⬇, and ⬆ to move to the desired cell location. Type in the number and press either the ENTER key or one of the cursor keys. Repeat this procedure until all the necessary input cells are filled.

Viewing the Spreadsheet Schedules and Graph

You can press the cursor keys (⬅, ➡, ⬇, and ⬆), or the Page Up PG↑ and the Page Down PG↓ keys to move around the worksheet area. Press the Home key to return to the upper left-hand corner of the spreadsheet.

The worksheet contains a graph. Click on the "Chart" tab to see the graph.

Saving the Spreadsheet

After entering your estimates and examining the results, including the graph, save your spreadsheet by using the following commands.

Keystrokes for Excel or 1-2-3W	Comments
ESC ESC	If the top of the display screen shows one of the command menus, (see the introduction section of the manual) press the Escape key until the menus disappear. Skip this step if a menu is not displayed.
ALT FS	Access the Command menu, the File menu and the Save option.
ENTER	Press Enter to save under the same name. An Excel file is saved with a "XLS" suffix, and a 1-2-3 for Windows file is saved as a "WK4" file.

Table 10-2:   Save REGRESS worksheet

Printing the Worksheet

Place the mouse cursor on top of the "Print Worksheet" button to print it, and click on the "Print Chart" button to print the graph. Make sure you have a printer connected and turned on before attempting to print your results.

Bring the results of your analysis to class when the case is discussed.

Input Form for REGRESS

Name _____

Title 1_____

Title 2_____

X Axis Title _____

Y Axis Title _____

Data Points   X   Y

Data Point #1   _____   _____

Data Point #2   _____   _____

Data Point #3   _____   _____

Data Point #4   _____   _____

Data Point #5   _____   _____

Data Point #6   _____   _____

Data Point #7   _____   _____

Data Point #8   _____   _____

Data Point #9   _____   _____

Data Point #10   _____   _____

Data Point #11   _____   _____

Data Point #12   _____   _____

Data Point #13   _____   _____

Data Point #14   _____   _____

Data Point #15   _____   _____

Data Point #16   _____   _____

Data Point #17   _____   _____

Data Point #18   _____   _____

Data Point #19   _____   _____

Output Form for REGRESS

Name _____

Results:

Intercept (a) =   _____

Slope (b) =   _____

Equation =   _____ + _____ *X

Correlation Coefficient   (R)   _____

Index of Determination   (R^2) =   _____

Standard Error of Residuals (Se) =   _____

Standard Error of Coefficient (Slope) (Sb) =   _____

T-Value =   _____

What-If Analysis:

Enter X value.   _____

Projected Y value.   _____ +/- 2 STD = _____

CHAPTER 11:
Pharmacia & Upjohn, Inc.:
Rogaine Hair Regrowth Treatment

Introduction

The U.S. Food and Drug Administration (FDA) approved Rogaine Hair Regrowth Treatment for sale without a physician's prescription. However, on April 30th, 1996 the company found that the FDA approved three competing generic products for sale without a prescription. The company must reevaluate its marketing plan. Now prospective users of the product could try a competitive product and current Rogaine users could switch to another product. The spreadsheet for this case provides insight into the impact on Rogaine sales based on different marketing strategies.

This worksheet has no graph.

How to Use the Worksheet

1.   Fill out the input form provided for this worksheet after reading the case you are analyzing.

2.   If you have not used any of the worksheets in this manual, please review the section of the manual on how to load Microsoft Excel or Lotus 1-2-3 for Windows, and the worksheets provided on the disk.

3.   Load the worksheet program. After the row and column format appears, load the worksheet using the keystrokes shown in the table below. See the section of the manual on how to load worksheets if you experience difficulties.

Keystrokes for Excel or 1-2-3W	Comments
[ALT] FO	Access the Command menu, the File menu and execute the Retrieve command.
ROGAINE	Either type in the file name, or highlight the name using the cursor keys, or mouse.
[ENTER]	Press the Enter key to load the worksheet.

Table 11-1:   Load ROGAINE worksheet

4.   After loading the worksheet, review it to make sure you know where the input cells are located. The input cells are colored differently than the rest of the cells on a color monitor. The first time you use the worksheet, most of the cells in the spreadsheet will display "NA", or "#NA", but don't worry. As you enter your input values, the NA's in the output cells will be replaced by calculated values.

Unless you have disabled the worksheet protection, only the input cells can be changed. If you accidentally attempt to change a protected (non-input) cell, the program will display an error message. Press the [ESC] key to return to normal operations.

The input sections of the worksheet for this case are boxed for emphasis in the figures below. Remember that the boxes do not show on the worksheet itself.

Worksheet

	A	B	C	D	E	F	G	H	I	J
1	Name = ROGAINE									
2										
3	Sales Projection of Rogaine With Generic Competition									
4	Projection for Men:									
5	Number of potential users in target market						#N/A			
6	Expenditure for First Time Trier						#N/A			
7	Percent Estimate for Repeat Triers						#N/A	%		
8	Expenditure for Repeater Triers						#N/A			
9										
10	Rogaine Sales Potential for Men: 1988-1995. (All dollar amount in Millions.)									
11	Year	Increm. Trial %	Cum. %	No. of 1st Time Triers	1st Time Trier Sales $ Mill.	No of Repeat Triers	Annual Repeat Trier Sales $ Mill.	Cum. Repeat Trier Sales $ Mill.	Total Annual Sales $ Mill.	Cum. Sales $ Mill.
12	1988	#N/A	#N/A	#N/A	#N/A	#N/A	#N/A	#N/A	#N/A	#N/A
13	1989	#N/A	#N/A	#N/A	#N/A	#N/A	#N/A	#N/A	#N/A	#N/A
14	1990	#N/A	#N/A	#N/A	#N/A	#N/A	#N/A	#N/A	#N/A	#N/A
15	1991	#N/A	#N/A	#N/A	#N/A	#N/A	#N/A	#N/A	#N/A	#N/A
16	1992	#N/A	#N/A	#N/A	#N/A	#N/A	#N/A	#N/A	#N/A	#N/A
17	1993	#N/A	#N/A	#N/A	#N/A	#N/A	#N/A	#N/A	#N/A	#N/A
18	1994	#N/A	#N/A	#N/A	#N/A	#N/A	#N/A	#N/A	#N/A	#N/A
19	1995	#N/A	#N/A	#N/A	#N/A	#N/A	#N/A	#N/A	#N/A	#N/A
20		Total		#N/A	#N/A	#N/A	#N/A	#N/A	#N/A	#N/A
21										
22	Sales Projection of Rogaine With Generic Competition									
23	Projection for Women:									
24	Number of potential users in target market						#N/A			
25	Expenditure for First Time Trier						#N/A			
26	Percent Estimate for Repeat Triers						#N/A	%		
27	Expenditure for Repeater Triers						#N/A			
28										
29	Rogaine Sales Potential for Women: 1992-1995. (All dollar amount in Millions.)									
30	Year	Increm. Trial %	Cum. %	No. of 1st Time Triers	1st Time Trier Sales $ Mill.	No of Repeat Triers	Annual Repeat Trier Sales $ Mill.	Cum. Repeat Trier Sales $ Mill.	Total Annual Sales $ Mill.	Cum. Sales $ Mill.
31	1992	#N/A	#N/A	#N/A	#N/A	#N/A	#N/A	#N/A	#N/A	#N/A
32	1993	#N/A	#N/A	#N/A	#N/A	#N/A	#N/A	#N/A	#N/A	#N/A
33	1994	#N/A	#N/A	#N/A	#N/A	#N/A	#N/A	#N/A	#N/A	#N/A
34	1995	#N/A	#N/A	#N/A	#N/A	#N/A	#N/A	#N/A	#N/A	#N/A
35		Total		#N/A	#N/A	#N/A	#N/A	#N/A	#N/A	#N/A
36										
37	Sales Projection of Rogaine Without Generic Competition									
38	Projection for Men:									
39	Number of potential users in target market						#N/A			
40	Expenditure for First Time Trier						#N/A			
41	Percent Estimate for Repeat Triers						#N/A	%		
42	Expenditure for Repeater Triers						#N/A			
43										
44	Rogaine Sales Potential for Men: 1996-2000. (All dollar amount in Millions.)									
45	Year	Increm. Trial %	Cum. %	No. of 1st Time Triers	1st Time Trier Sales $ Mill.	No of Repeat Triers	Annual Repeat Trier Sales $ Mill.	Cum. Repeat Trier Sales $ Mill.	Total Annual Sales $ Mill.	Cum. Sales $ Mill.
46	1996	#N/A	#N/A	#N/A	#N/A	#N/A	#N/A	#N/A	#N/A	#N/A
47	1997	#N/A	#N/A	#N/A	#N/A	#N/A	#N/A	#N/A	#N/A	#N/A
48	1998	#N/A	#N/A	#N/A	#N/A	#N/A	#N/A	#N/A	#N/A	#N/A
49	1999	#N/A	#N/A	#N/A	#N/A	#N/A	#N/A	#N/A	#N/A	#N/A
50	2000	#N/A	#N/A	#N/A	#N/A	#N/A	#N/A	#N/A	#N/A	#N/A
51		Total		#N/A	#N/A	#N/A	#N/A	#N/A	#N/A	#N/A

Worksheet -- Continued

	A	B	C	D	E	F	G	H	I	J
52										
53	Sales Projection of Rogaine Without Generic Competition									
54	Projection for Women:									
55	Number of potential users in target market						#N/A			
56	Expenditure for First Time Trier						#N/A			
57	Percent Estimate for Repeat Triers						#N/A	%		
58	Expenditure for Repeater Triers						#N/A			
59										
60	Rogaine Sales Potential for Women: 1996-2000. (All dollar amount in Millions.)									
61	Year	Increm. Trial %	Cum. %	No. of 1st Time Triers	1st Time Trier Sales $ Mill.	No of Repeat Triers	Annual Repeat Trier Sales $ Mill.	Cum. Repeat Trier Sales $ Mill.	Total Annual Sales $ Mill.	Cum. Sales $ Mill.
62	1996	#N/A	#N/A	#N/A	#N/A	#N/A	#N/A	#N/A	#N/A	#N/A
63	1997	#N/A	#N/A	#N/A	#N/A	#N/A	#N/A	#N/A	#N/A	#N/A
64	1998	#N/A	#N/A	#N/A	#N/A	#N/A	#N/A	#N/A	#N/A	#N/A
65	1999	#N/A	#N/A	#N/A	#N/A	#N/A	#N/A	#N/A	#N/A	#N/A
66	2000	#N/A	#N/A	#N/A	#N/A	#N/A	#N/A	#N/A	#N/A	#N/A
67	Total			#N/A	#N/A	#N/A	#N/A	#N/A	#N/A	#N/A

5.   Type into the spreadsheet your estimates of the inputs using the information from the input forms you filled out in Step 1. Use the cursor keys ⬅, ➡, ⬇, and ⬆ to move to the desired cell location. Type in the number and press either the [ENTER] key or one of the cursor keys. Repeat this procedure until all the necessary input cells are filled.

Viewing the Spreadsheet Schedules and Graph

You can press the cursor keys (⬅, ➡, ⬇, and ⬆), or the Page Up [PG↑] and the Page Down [PG↓] keys to move around the worksheet area. Press the Home key to return to the upper left-hand corner of the spreadsheet.

The worksheet contains a graph. Click on the "Chart" tab to see the graph.

Saving the Spreadsheet

After entering your estimates and examining the results, including the graph, save your spreadsheet by using the following commands.

Keystrokes for Excel or 1-2-3W	Comments
[ESC] [ESC]	If the top of the display screen shows one of the command menus, (see the introduction section of the manual) press the Escape key until the menus disappear. Skip this step if a menu is not displayed.
[ALT] FS	Access the Command menu, the File menu and the Save option.
[ENTER]	Press Enter to save under the same name. An Excel file is saved with a "XLS" suffix, and a 1-2-3 for Windows file is saved as a "WK4" file.

Table 11-2:   Save ROGAINE worksheet

Printing the Worksheet

Place the mouse cursor on top of the "Print Worksheet" button to print it, and click on the "Print Chart" button to print the graph. Make sure you have a printer connected and turned on before attempting to print your results.

Bring the results of your analysis to class when the case is discussed.

Input Form for ROGAINE

Input for all options:

	With Generic Competition		Without Generic Competition	
	Men	Women	Men	Women
Number of potential users in target market	_____	_____	_____	_____
Expenditure for First Time Trier	_____	_____	_____	_____
Percent Estimate for Repeat Triers	_____	_____	_____	_____
Expenditure for Repeater Triers	_____	_____	_____	_____

Input for generic competition trial percentages:

Incremental Trial Percentages:

Year	With Generic Competition	
	Men	Women
1988	_____	
1989	_____	
1990	_____	
1991	_____	
1992	_____	_____
1993	_____	_____
1994	_____	_____
1995	_____	_____

Input for without generic competition trial percentages:

Incremental Trial Percentages:

Year	Without Generic Competition	
	Men	Women
1996	_____	_____
1997	_____	_____
1998	_____	_____
1999	_____	_____
2000	_____	_____

Output Form for ROGAINE

Sales Projections of Rogaine With Generic Competition:

Total Annual Sales in Millions

Year	Men	Women
1988		
1989		
1990		
1991		
1992		
1993		
1994		
1995		

Sales Projections of Rogaine Without Generic Competition:

Total Annual Sales in Millions

Year	Men	Women
1996		
1997		
1998		
1999		
2000		

Chapter 12:
South Delaware Coors, Inc.

Introduction

Larry Brownlow is considering starting his own small business. He must first decide what market research will help him with his decision on the Coors distributorship. The preparation of pro forma income statements will provide assistance to Larry in making his decision.

How to Use the Worksheet

1.   Fill out the input form provided for this worksheet after reading the case you are analyzing.

2.   If you have not used any of the worksheets in this manual, please review the section of the manual on how to load Microsoft Excel or Lotus 1-2-3 for Windows, and the worksheets provided on the disk.

3.   Load the worksheet program. After the row and column format appears, load the worksheet using the keystrokes shown in the table below. See the section of the manual on how to load worksheets if you experience difficulties.

Keystrokes for Excel or 1-2-3W	Comments
[ALT] FO	Access the Command menu, the File menu and execute the Retrieve command.
COORS	Either type in the file name, or highlight the name using the cursor keys, or mouse.
[ENTER]	Press the Enter key to load the worksheet.

Table 12-1:   Load COORS worksheet

4.   After loading the worksheet, review it to make sure you know where the input cells are located. The input cells are colored differently than the rest of the cells on a color monitor. The first time you use the worksheet, most of the cells in the spreadsheet will display "NA", or "#NA", but don't worry. As you enter your input values, the NA's in the output cells will be replaced by calculated values.

Unless you have disabled the worksheet protection, only the input cells can be changed. If you accidentally attempt to change a protected (non-input) cell, the program will display an error message. Press the [ESC] key to return to normal operations.

The input sections of the worksheet for this case are boxed for emphasis in the figures below. Remember that the boxes do not show on the worksheet itself.

Worksheet

	A	B	C	D	E	F
1	Name = COORS					
2						
3	INPUT FORM					
4	SOUTH DELAWARE COORS, INC				OPTIMISTIC	PESSIMISTIC
5					OPTION	OPTION
6	MARKET ESTIMATES:					
7	Total Market Size (Gallons)				#N/A	#N/A
8	Mkt. Growth Rate Per Year (%)				#N/A	#N/A
9	PRICE PER GALLON:				#N/A	#N/A
10	COST OF GOODS SOLD (% OF SALES)				#N/A	#N/A
11	GROSS MARGIN (% OF SALES)				#N/A	#N/A
12	FIXED COST PER YEAR:					
13	Salaries				#N/A	#N/A
14	Depreciation				#N/A	#N/A
15	Utilities & Telephone				#N/A	#N/A
16	Insurance				#N/A	#N/A
17	Interest on Loan				#N/A	#N/A
18	Property Taxes				#N/A	#N/A
19	Maintenance				#N/A	#N/A
20	Travel and Advertising				#N/A	#N/A
21	Miscellaneous				#N/A	#N/A
22	CAPITAL INVESTMENT:					
23	Accounts Receivable				#N/A	#N/A
24	Inventory				#N/A	#N/A
25	Equipment				#N/A	#N/A
26	Warehouse				#N/A	#N/A
27	Land				#N/A	#N/A
28	FUNDING SOURCES:					
29	Personal Loans				#N/A	#N/A
30	Family Loans				#N/A	#N/A
31	Bank Loans				#N/A	#N/A
32	ESTIMATED FIRM MARKET SHARE:					
33	Year 1 Enter As Percent				#N/A	#N/A
34	Year 2 Enter As Percent				#N/A	#N/A
35	Year 3 Enter As Percent				#N/A	#N/A
36						

5.   Type into the spreadsheet your estimates of the inputs using the information from the input forms you filled out in Step 1. Use the cursor keys ⬅, ➡, ⬇, and ⬆ to move to the desired cell location. Type in the number and press either the ENTER key or one of the cursor keys. Repeat this procedure until all the necessary input cells are filled.

Viewing the Spreadsheet Schedules and Graph

You can press the cursor keys ([←], [→], [↓], and [↑]), or the Page Up [PG↑] and the Page Down [PG↓] keys to move around the worksheet area. Press the Home key to return to the upper left-hand corner of the spreadsheet.

The worksheet contains a graph. Click on the "Chart" tab to see the graph.

Saving the Spreadsheet

After entering your estimates and examining the results, including the graph, save your spreadsheet by using the following commands.

Keystrokes for Excel or 1-2-3W	Comments
[ESC] [ESC]	If the top of the display screen shows one of the command menus, (see the introduction section of the manual) press the Escape key until the menus disappear. Skip this step if a menu is not displayed.
[ALT] FS	Access the Command menu, the File menu and the Save option.
[ENTER]	Press Enter to save under the same name. An Excel file is saved with a "XLS" suffix, and a 1-2-3 for Windows file is saved as a "WK4" file.

Table 12-2:   Save COORS worksheet

Printing the Worksheet

Place the mouse cursor on top of the "Print Worksheet" button to print it, and click on the "Print Chart" button to print the graph. Make sure you have a printer connected and turned on before attempting to print your results.

Bring the results of your analysis to class when the case is discussed.

Input Form for COORS - Page 1 of 2

Name _____

```
        SOUTH DELAWARE COORS, INC
              INPUT FORM               OPTIMISTIC  PESSIMISTIC
                                         OPTION      OPTION
                                       _____  _____


  MARKET ESTIMATES:
        TOTAL MARKET SIZE (GALLONS)   _____  _____

        MKT GROWTH RATE PER YEAR (%)  _____  _____

PRICE PER GALLON:                     _____  _____

  COST OF GOODS SOLD (% OF SALES)      ̶1̶6̶0̶,̶0̶0̶0̶    ̶1̶6̶0̶,̶0̶0̶0̶

  FIXED COST PER YEAR:
        SALARIES                       160,000     160,000

      DEPRECIATION                      50,000      50,000

      UTILITIES & TELE                  12,000      12,000

      INSURANCE                         10,000      10,000

      INTEREST ON LOAN                _____  _____

      PROPERTY TAXES                    10,000      10,000

      MAINTENANCE                        5,600       5,600

      TRAVEL AND ADVERTISING          _____  _____

      MISCELLANEOUS                      2,400    _____

ESTIMATED FIRM MARKET SHARE:
        YEAR 1   (ENTER AS PERCENT)   _____  _____

        YEAR 2   (ENTER AS PERCENT)   _____  _____

        YEAR 3   (ENTER AS PERCENT)   _____  _____
```

Output Form for COORS - Page 1 of 2

Name _____

OPTIMISTIC PROJECTIONS:

SOUTH DELAWARE COORS, INC
PRO FORMA INCOME STATEMENT

	YEAR 1	YEAR 2	YEAR 3
SALES	_____	_____	_____
COST OF GOODS SOLD	_____	_____	_____
GROSS PROFIT	_____	_____	_____
OPERATING EXPENSES: SALARIES	_____	_____	_____
DEPRECIATION	_____	_____	_____
UTILITIES & TEL	_____	_____	_____
INSURANCE	_____	_____	_____
INTEREST ON LOAN	_____	_____	_____
PROPERTY TAXES	_____	_____	_____
MAINTENANCE	_____	_____	_____
TRAVEL AND ADVERTISING	_____	_____	_____
MISCELLANEOUS	_____	_____	_____
TOTAL OPERATING EXP.	_____	_____	_____
NET INCOME FROM OPERATIONS	_____	_____	_____
ESTIMATED INCOME TAXES	_____	_____	_____
NET INCOME AFTER TAX	_____	_____	_____

Output Form for COORS - Page 2 of 2

PESSIMISTIC PROJECTIONS:

SOUTH DELAWARE COORS, INC
PRO FORMA INCOME STATEMENT

	YEAR 1	YEAR 2	YEAR 3
SALES	_____	_____	_____
COST OF GOODS SOLD	_____	_____	_____
GROSS PROFIT	_____	_____	_____
OPERATING EXPENSES: SALARIES	_____	_____	_____
DEPRECIATION	_____	_____	_____
UTILITIES & TEL	_____	_____	_____
INSURANCE	_____	_____	_____
INTEREST ON LOAN	_____	_____	_____
PROPERTY TAXES	_____	_____	_____
MAINTENANCE	_____	_____	_____
TRAVEL AND ADVERTISING	_____	_____	_____
MISCELLANEOUS	_____	_____	_____
TOTAL OPERATING EXP.	_____	_____	_____
NET INCOME FROM OPERATIONS	_____	_____	_____
ESTIMATED INCOME TAXES	_____	_____	_____
NET INCOME AFTER TAX	_____	_____	_____

Chapter 13:
Soft and Silky Shaving Gel

Introduction

Phoebe Masters, product manager for hand and body lotions at Ms-Tique Corporation, is faced with a decision on whether to add a 5 1/2-ounce or 10-ounce aerosol package to the Soft and Silky shaving gel line. Test market information which provides low and high estimates of sales potential has been collected to assist Phoebe Masters in this decision.

How to Use the Worksheet

1.   Fill out the input form provided for this worksheet after reading the case you are analyzing.

2.   If you have not used any of the worksheets in this manual, please review the section of the manual on how to load Microsoft Excel or Lotus 1-2-3 for Windows, and the worksheets provided on the disk.

3.   Load the worksheet program. After the row and column format appears, load the worksheet using the keystrokes shown in the table below. See the section of the manual on how to load worksheets if you experience difficulties.

Keystrokes for Excel or 1-2-3W	Comments
[ALT] FO	Access the Command menu, the File menu and execute the Retrieve command.
SOFT	Either type in the file name, or highlight the name using the cursor keys, or mouse.
[ENTER]	Press the Enter key to load the worksheet.
Table 13-1: Load SOFT worksheet	

4.   After loading the worksheet, review it to make sure you know where the input cells are located. The input cells are colored differently than the rest of the cells on a color monitor. The first time you use the worksheet, most of the cells in the spreadsheet will display "NA", or "#NA", but don't worry. As you enter your input values, the NA's in the output cells will be replaced by calculated values.

Unless you have disabled the worksheet protection, only the input cells can be changed. If you accidentally attempt to change a protected (non-input) cell, the program will display an error message. Press the [ESC] key to return to normal operations.

The input sections of the worksheet for this case are boxed for emphasis in the figures below. Remember that the boxes do not show on the worksheet itself.

Worksheet

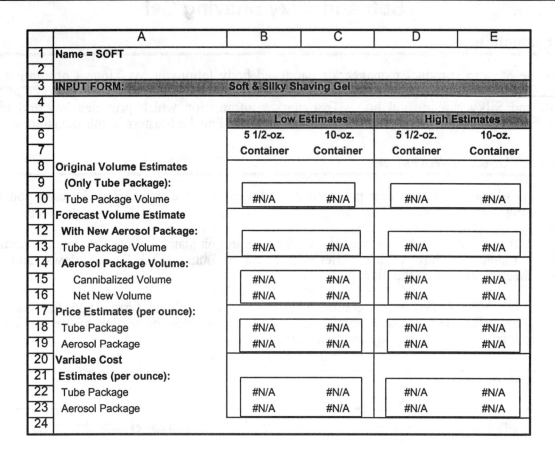

5.   Type into the spreadsheet your estimates of the inputs using the information from the input forms you filled out in Step 1. Use the cursor keys ⬅, ➡, ⬇, and ⬆ to move to the desired cell location. Type in the number and press either the ⏎ENTER key or one of the cursor keys. Repeat this procedure until all the necessary input cells are filled.

Viewing the Spreadsheet Schedules and Graph

You can press the cursor keys (⬅, ➡, ⬇, and ⬆), or the Page Up ⬆PG and the Page Down ⬇PG keys to move around the worksheet area. Press the Home key to return to the upper left-hand corner of the spreadsheet.

The worksheet contains a graph. Click on the "Chart" tab to see the graph.

Saving the Spreadsheet

After entering your estimates and examining the results, including the graph, save your spreadsheet by using the following commands.

Keystrokes for Excel or 1-2-3W	Comments
[ESC] [ESC]	If the top of the display screen shows one of the command menus, (see the introduction section of the manual) press the Escape key until the menus disappear. Skip this step if a menu is not displayed.
[ALT] FS	Access the Command menu, the File menu and the Save option.
[ENTER]	Press Enter to save under the same name. An Excel file is saved with a "XLS" suffix, and a 1-2-3 for Windows file is saved as a "WK4" file.

Table 13-2:   Save SOFT worksheet

Printing the Worksheet

Place the mouse cursor on top of the "Print Worksheet" button to print it, and click on the "Print Chart" button to print the graph. Make sure you have a printer connected and turned on before attempting to print your results.

Bring the results of your analysis to class when the case is discussed.

Input Form for SOFT

Name _____

SOFT INPUT FORM

INPUT FORM:	Low Estimates 5 1/2-oz. Container	10-oz. Container	High Estimates 5 1/2-oz. Container	10-oz. Container
Original Volume Estimates (Only Tube Package): Tube Package Volume	_____	_____	_____	_____
Forecast Volume Estimate With New Aerosol Package: Tube Package Volume	_____	_____	_____	_____
Aerosol Package Volume: Cannibalized Volume	_____	_____	_____	_____
Net New Volume	_____	_____	_____	_____
Price Estimates (per ounce): Tube Package	_____	_____	_____	_____
Aerosol Package	_____	_____	_____	_____
Variable Cost Estimates (per ounce): Tube Package	_____	_____	_____	_____
Aerosol Package	_____	_____	_____	_____

Output Form for SOFT

Name _____

Changes in Sales, Variable Costs, and Contribution with New Aerosol Package Addition

Low Estimates:	5.5-oz. Container			10-oz. Container		
	Unit Volume	Unit contribution	Total Contribution Dollars	Unit Volume	Unit contribution	Total Contribution Dollars
Forecast Volume - Tube Pkg. Aerosol Package:	_____	_____	_____	_____	_____	_____
Cannibalized Volume	_____	_____	_____	_____	_____	_____
Incremental Volume	_____	_____	_____	_____	_____	_____
Total	_____	_____	_____	_____	_____	_____
Less: Original forecase vol. for tube pkg.	_____		_____	_____		_____
Total Change	_____		_____	_____		_____

High Estimates:	5.5-oz. Container			10-oz. Container		
	Unit Volume	Unit contriution	Total Contribution Dollars	Unit Volume	Unit contribution	Total Contribution Dollars
Forecast Volume - Tube Pkg. Aerosol Package:	_____	_____	_____	_____	_____	_____
Cannibalized Volume Incremental Volume	_____	_____	_____	_____	_____	_____
	_____	_____	_____	_____	_____	_____
Total	_____	_____	_____	_____	_____	_____
Less: Original forecase vol. for tube pkg.	_____		_____	_____		_____
Total Change	_____		_____	_____		_____

Chapter 14:
Frito-Lay's Dips

Introduction

Frito-Lay executives had just completed the planning review for Frito-Lay's Dips. The major issue raised was where and how Frito-Lay's Dips could be developed further. Several viewpoints were presented. One position was that Frito-Lay should pursue a market penetration strategy and build market share in the "chip dip" category where it has an excellent market position. Another viewpoint was that Frito-Lay should pursue a market development strategy using its new sour cream-based dip to enter the "vegetable dip" category.

The worksheet provided for this case computes pro forma income statements based on your estimates of key values for the dip categories. Therefore, you can evaluate different strategies in terms of their impact on the profit contribution. The worksheet calculates the profit contribution and profit percentage for dips.

How to Use the Worksheet

1.   Fill out the input form provided for this worksheet after reading the case you are analyzing.

2.   If you have not used any of the worksheets in this manual, please review the section of the manual on how to load Microsoft Excel or Lotus 1-2-3 for Windows, and the worksheets provided on the disk.

3.   Load the worksheet program. After the row and column format appears, load the worksheet using the keystrokes shown in the table below. See the section of the manual on how to load worksheets if you experience difficulties.

Keystrokes for Excel or 1-2-3W	Comments
[ALT] FO	Access the Command menu, the File menu and execute the Retrieve command.
FRITO	Either type in the file name, or highlight the name using the cursor keys, or mouse.
[ENTER]	Press the Enter key to load the worksheet.

Table 14-1:   Load FRITO worksheet

4.   After loading the worksheet, review it to make sure you know where the input cells are located. The input cells are colored differently than the rest of the cells on a color monitor. The first time you use the worksheet, most of the cells in the spreadsheet will display "NA", or "#NA", but don't worry. As you enter your input values, the NA's in the output cells will be replaced by calculated values.

Unless you have disabled the worksheet protection, only the input cells can be changed. If you accidentally attempt to change a protected (non-input) cell, the program will display an error message. Press the [ESC] key to return to normal operations.

The input sections of the worksheet for this case are boxed for emphasis in the figures below. Remember that the boxes do not show on the worksheet itself.

Worksheet

	A	B	C	D	E	F	G
1	Name = FRITO						
2							
3		Frito-Lay's Dips 1986 Sales, Expense and Profit Forecast					
4		All dollars in thousands ($000's)					
5						Sour	
6				Mexican	Cheese	Cream	Total
7				Dips	Dips	Dip	Dips
8	Net Sales			#N/A	#N/A	#N/A	#N/A
9	Gross Margin			#N/A	#N/A	#N/A	#N/A
10	Marketing Expense:						
11	Selling			#N/A	#N/A	#N/A	#N/A
12	Freight			#N/A	#N/A	#N/A	#N/A
13	Cons. Adv.			#N/A	#N/A	#N/A	#N/A
14	Cons. & Trade Promo			#N/A	#N/A	#N/A	#N/A
15	Total Marketing Expense			#N/A	#N/A	#N/A	#N/A
16	General & Admin Overhead			#N/A	#N/A	#N/A	#N/A
17	Total Expenses			#N/A	#N/A	#N/A	#N/A
18	Profit Contribution			#N/A	#N/A	#N/A	#N/A
19							
20	Profit Percentage			#N/A	#N/A	#N/A	#N/A
21							

5.   Type into the spreadsheet your estimates of the inputs using the information from the input forms you filled out in Step 1. Use the cursor keys ⬅, ➡, ⬇, and ⬆ to move to the desired cell location. Type in the number and press either the ENTER key or one of the cursor keys. Repeat this procedure until all the necessary input cells are filled.

Viewing the Spreadsheet Schedules and Graph

You can press the cursor keys (⬅, ➡, ⬇, and ⬆), or the Page Up PG↑ and the Page Down PG↓ keys to move around the worksheet area. Press the Home key to return to the upper left-hand corner of the spreadsheet.

The worksheet contains a graph. Click on the "Chart" tab to see the graph.

Saving the Spreadsheet

After entering your estimates and examining the results, including the graph, save your spreadsheet by using the following commands.

Keystrokes for Excel or 1-2-3W	Comments
[ESC] [ESC]	If the top of the display screen shows one of the command menus, (see the introduction section of the manual) press the Escape key until the menus disappear. Skip this step if a menu is not displayed.
[ALT] FS	Access the Command menu, the File menu and the Save option.
[ENTER]	Press Enter to save under the same name. An Excel file is saved with a "XLS" suffix, and a 1-2-3 for Windows file is saved as a "WK4" file.

Table 14-2: Save FRITO worksheet

Printing the Worksheet

Place the mouse cursor on top of the "Print Worksheet" button to print it, and click on the "Print Chart" button to print the graph. Make sure you have a printer connected and turned on before attempting to print your results.

Bring the results of your analysis to class when the case is discussed.

Input Form for Frito-Lay's Dips

Name _____

Frito-Lay's Dips 1986 Sales, Expense and Profit Forecast
All dollars in thousands ($000's)

	Mexican Dips	Cheese Dips	Sour Cream Dip	Total Dips
Net Sales	_____	_____	_____	_____
Gross Margin	_____	_____	_____	_____
Marketing Expense:				
Selling	_____	_____	_____	_____
Freight	_____	_____	_____	_____
Cons. Adv.	_____	_____	_____	_____
Cons. & Trade Promo	_____	_____	_____	_____
General & Admin.				
Overhead	_____	_____	_____	_____

Output Form for Frito-Lay's Dips

Name _____

Frito-Lay's Dips 1986 Sales, Expense and Profit Forecast
All dollars in thousands ($000's)

	Mexican Dips	Cheese Dips	Sour Cream Dip	Total Dips
Net Sales	_____	_____	_____	_____
Gross Margin	_____	_____	_____	_____
Marketing Expense:				
Selling	_____	_____	_____	_____
Freight	_____	_____	_____	_____
Cons. Adv.	_____	_____	_____	_____
Cons. & Trade Promo	_____	_____	_____	_____
Total Marketing Expense	_____	_____	_____	_____
General & Admin Overhead	_____	_____	_____	_____
Total Expenses	_____	_____	_____	_____
Profit Contribution	_____	_____	_____	_____
Profit Percentage	_____	_____	_____	_____

Chapter 15:
Perpetual Care Hospital: Downtown Health Clinic

Introduction

The assistant administrator at the Perpetual Care Hospital and the Director of the Downtown Health Clinic (DHC) became aware of a market study being performed in the DHC service area by a major competitor. This competitor- Medcenter - is an aggressive, market-oriented, privately owned clinic. The administrator has been asked to perform an analysis of DHC's position and evaluate possible alternatives. These alternatives include: doing nothing; expanding hours, adding gynecology services, or some combination of alternatives.

How to Use the Worksheet

1.   Fill out the input form provided for this worksheet after reading the case you are analyzing.

2.   If you have not used any of the worksheets in this manual, please review the section of the manual on how to load Microsoft Excel or Lotus 1-2-3 for Windows, and the worksheets provided on the disk.

3.   Load the worksheet program. After the row and column format appears, load the worksheet using the keystrokes shown in the table below. See the section of the manual on how to load worksheets if you experience difficulties.

Keystrokes for Excel or 1-2-3W	Comments
[ALT] FO	Access the Command menu, the File menu and execute the Retrieve command.
HOSPITAL	Either type in the file name, or highlight the name using the cursor keys, or mouse.
[ENTER]	Press the Enter key to load the worksheet.

Table 15-1:   Load HOSPITAL worksheet

4.   After loading the worksheet, review it to make sure you know where the input cells are located. The input cells are colored differently than the rest of the cells on a color monitor. The first time you use the worksheet, most of the cells in the spreadsheet will display "NA", or "#NA", but don't worry. As you enter your input values, the NA's in the output cells will be replaced by calculated values.

Unless you have disabled the worksheet protection, only the input cells can be changed. If you accidentally attempt to change a protected (non-input) cell, the program will display an error message. Press the [ESC] key to return to normal operations.

The input sections of the worksheet for this case are boxed for emphasis in the figures below. Remember that the boxes do not show on the worksheet itself.

Worksheet

	A	B	C	D	E	F	G
1	Name = HOSPITAL						
2							
3	Perpetual Care Hospital Input Form						
4				OPTIONS			
5				Do Nothing	Expand Hours	Gynecologist	Comb.
6				Option	Option	Option	Option
7	Projected Visits:						
8	Personal Illness/Exams			#N/A	#N/A	#N/A	#N/A
9	Worker's Compensation			#N/A	#N/A	#N/A	#N/A
10	Employment/Insur. Exam			#N/A	#N/A	#N/A	#N/A
11	Emergency			#N/A	#N/A	#N/A	#N/A
12	Gynecology			#N/A	#N/A	#N/A	#N/A
13	Total Visits						
14	Average Prices/Visit:						
15	Personal Illness/Exams			#N/A	#N/A	#N/A	#N/A
16	Worker's Compensation			#N/A	#N/A	#N/A	#N/A
17	Employment/Insur. Exam			#N/A	#N/A	#N/A	#N/A
18	Emergency			#N/A	#N/A	#N/A	#N/A
19	Gynecology			#N/A	#N/A	#N/A	#N/A
20							
21	Variable Costs (as a % of Sales):			#N/A	#N/A	#N/A	#N/A
22	Fixed Costs/Year:						
23	Personnel			#N/A	#N/A	#N/A	#N/A
24	Professional Services			#N/A	#N/A	#N/A	#N/A
25	Gynecologist			#N/A	#N/A	#N/A	#N/A
26	Facility & Miscellaneous			#N/A	#N/A	#N/A	#N/A
27	Amortization			#N/A	#N/A	#N/A	#N/A
28							

5.   Type into the spreadsheet your estimates of the inputs using the information from the input forms you filled out in Step 1. Use the cursor keys ⬅, ➡, ⬇, and ⬆ to move to the desired cell location. Type in the number and press either the ⏎ ENTER key or one of the cursor keys. Repeat this procedure until all the necessary input cells are filled.

Viewing the Spreadsheet Schedules and Graph

You can press the cursor keys (⬅, ➡, ⬇, and ⬆), or the Page Up PG↑ and the Page Down PG↓ keys to move around the worksheet area. Press the Home key to return to the upper left-hand corner of the spreadsheet.

The worksheet contains a graph. Click on the "Chart" tab to see the graph.

Saving the Spreadsheet

After entering your estimates and examining the results, including the graph, save your spreadsheet by using the following commands.

Keystrokes for Excel or 1-2-3W	Comments
[ESC] [ESC]	If the top of the display screen shows one of the command menus, (see the introduction section of the manual) press the Escape key until the menus disappear. Skip this step if a menu is not displayed.
[ALT] FS	Access the Command menu, the File menu and the Save option.
[ENTER]	Press Enter to save under the same name. An Excel file is saved with a "XLS" suffix, and a 1-2-3 for Windows file is saved as a "WK4" file.

Table 15-2:   Save HOSPITAL worksheet

Printing the Worksheet

Place the mouse cursor on top of the "Print Worksheet" button to print it, and click on the "Print Chart" button to print the graph. Make sure you have a printer connected and turned on before attempting to print your results.

Bring the results of your analysis to class when the case is discussed.

Input Form for HOSPITAL

Name _____

PERPETUAL CARE HOSPITAL: DOWNTOWN CLINIC
INPUT FORM

	--------- Options -------------------			
	Nothing Option	Exp. Hrs. Option	Gynecol. Option	Comb. Option
Projected Visits:				
Personal Illness/Exams	_____	_____	_____	_____
Worker's Compensation	_____	_____	_____	_____
Employment/Insur. Exam	_____	_____	_____	_____
Emergency	_____	_____	_____	_____
Gynecology	_____	_____	_____	_____
Average Prices/Visit: Personal Illness/Exams	_____	_____	_____	_____
Worker's Compensation	_____	_____	_____	_____
Employment/Insur. Exam	_____	_____	_____	_____
Emergency	_____	_____	_____	_____
Gynecology	_____	_____	_____	_____
Variable Costs (as a % of Sales)	_____	_____	_____	_____
Fixed Costs/Year: Personnel	_____	_____	_____	_____
Professional Services	_____	_____	_____	_____
Gynecologist	_____	_____	_____	_____
Facility & Miscellaneous	_____	_____	_____	_____
Amortization	_____	_____	_____	_____

Printing The Worksheet

You can print the worksheet in Lotus 1-2-3 for DOS by holding the [ALT] key down and pressing the "P" key. Print the worksheet in Microsoft Excel or Lotus 1-2-3 for Windows by holding down the [CTRL] key and pressing the "P" key. Make sure you have a printer connected and turned on before attempting to print your results.

Bring the results of your analysis to class when the case is discussed.

Output Form for HOSPITAL

Name _____

```
       PERPETUAL CARE HOSPITAL: DOWNTOWN CLINIC
              PROJECTED INCOME STATEMENTS
```

	Nothing Option	Exp. Hrs. Option	Gynecol. Option	Comb. Option
Gross Revenue				
Less: Variable Costs				
Contribution				
Less Fixed Expenses: Personnel				
Professional Services				
Gynecologist				
Facility & Misc.				
Amortization				
Total Fixed Expenses				
Net Income or Loss				

Chapter 16:
Swisher Mower and Machine Company

Introduction

In 1990, Max Swisher received an inquiry from a major national retail merchandise chain. The chain wanted to purchase Swisher Mower and Machine Company mowers and sell them under the retail chain's private label. Mr. Swisher, President of the company, must evaluate the chain's proposal.

How to Use the Worksheet

1.   Fill out the input form provided for this worksheet after reading the case you are analyzing.

2.   If you have not used any of the worksheets in this manual, please review the section of the manual on how to load Microsoft Excel or Lotus 1-2-3 for Windows, and the worksheets provided on the disk.

3.   Load the worksheet program. After the row and column format appears, load the worksheet using the keystrokes shown in the table below. See the section of the manual on how to load worksheets if you experience difficulties.

Keystrokes for Excel or 1-2-3W	Comments
[ALT] FO	Access the Command menu, the File menu and execute the Retrieve command.
SWISHER	Either type in the file name, or highlight the name using the cursor keys, or mouse.
[ENTER]	Press the Enter key to load the worksheet.

Table 16-1:   Load SWISHER worksheet

4.   After loading the worksheet, review it to make sure you know where the input cells are located. The input cells are colored differently than the rest of the cells on a color monitor. The first time you use the worksheet, most of the cells in the spreadsheet will display "NA", or "#NA", but don't worry. As you enter your input values, the NA's in the output cells will be replaced by calculated values.

Unless you have disabled the worksheet protection, only the input cells can be changed. If you accidentally attempt to change a protected (non-input) cell, the program will display an error message. Press the [ESC] key to return to normal operations.

The input sections of the worksheet for this case are boxed for emphasis in the figures below. Remember that the boxes do not show on the worksheet itself.

Worksheet

	A	B
1	Name = SWISHER	
2		
3		
4	Swisher Mower and Machine Company	
5	Input for Proposal Pro Forma Statement:	
6	Number of units sold	#N/A
7	Selling price per unit	#N/A
8	Normal direct labor costs per unit	#N/A
9	Normal direct material costs per unit	#N/A
10	Additional Incremental Costs:	
11	Direct material cost per unit	#N/A
12	Direct labor cost per unit	#N/A
13	Overhead per unit	#N/A
14	Other relevant costs per unit	#N/A
15	Number of units at regular gross	
16	profit lost if proposal accepted	#N/A
17	Gross profit on lost unit sales per unit	#N/A
18	Asset carrying costs for	
19	accounts receivable - total dollars	#N/A
20	Inventory carrying costs - total dollars	#N/A
21	Other one time costs associated with proposal	#N/A
22		

5.   Type into the spreadsheet your estimates of the inputs using the information from the input forms you filled out in Step 1. Use the cursor keys ⬅, ➡, ⬇, and ⬆ to move to the desired cell location. Type in the number and press either the ENTER key or one of the cursor keys. Repeat this procedure until all the necessary input cells are filled.

Viewing the Spreadsheet Schedules and Graph

You can press the cursor keys (⬅, ➡, ⬇, and ⬆), or the Page Up PG↑ and the Page Down PG↓ keys to move around the worksheet area. Press the Home key to return to the upper left-hand corner of the spreadsheet.

The worksheet contains a graph. Click on the "Chart" tab to see the graph.

Saving the Spreadsheet

After entering your estimates and examining the results, including the graph, save your spreadsheet by using the following commands.

Keystrokes for Excel or 1-2-3W	Comments
ESC **ESC**	If the top of the display screen shows one of the command menus, (see the introduction section of the manual) press the Escape key until the menus disappear. Skip this step if a menu is not displayed.
ALT FS	Access the Command menu, the File menu and the Save option.
ENTER	Press Enter to save under the same name. An Excel file is saved with a "XLS" suffix, and a 1-2-3 for Windows file is saved as a "WK4" file.

Table 16-2:   Save SWISHER worksheet

Printing the Worksheet

Place the mouse cursor on top of the "Print Worksheet" button to print it, and click on the "Print Chart" button to print the graph. Make sure you have a printer connected and turned on before attempting to print your results.

Bring the results of your analysis to class when the case is discussed.

Input Form for SWISHER

Name _____

Swisher Mower and Machine Company
Input for Proposal Pro Forma Statement:

Number of units sold $_____

Selling price per unit $_____

Normal direct labor costs per unit $_____

Normal direct material costs per unit $_____

Additional Incremental Costs:
   Direct material cost per unit $_____

   Direct labor cost per unit $_____

   Overhead per unit $_____

   Other relevant costs per unit $_____

   Number of units at regular gross
     profit lost if proposal accepted   _____

Gross profit on lost unit sales per unit $_____

Asset carrying costs for
   accounts receivable - total dollars $_____

Inventory carrying costs - total dollars $_____

Other one time costs associated with proposal $_____

Output Form for SWISHER

Swisher Mower and Machine Company

Pro Forma Statement on Private Brand Proposal

Revenue $_____

Cost of Goods Sold:
   Current Direct Labor $_____

   Current Direct Material   _____

   Incremental Direct Material   _____

   Incremental Direct Labor   _____

   Overhead   _____

   Other   _____

   Total Cost of Goods Sold   _____

Gross Profit/Margin $_____

Lost Gross Profit From Lost Sales   _____

Incremental Carrying Costs:
   Accounts Receivable $_____

   Inventory   _____

   Total $_____

Other One Time Costs   _____

Incremental Profit of Private Brand Proposal $_____

Chapter 17:
Carrington Furniture, Inc. (B)

Introduction

The 1996 merger between Carrington Furniture, Inc. and Lea-Meadows, Inc. has raised the issue of how to sell the Lea-Meadows product line. The selling of the Lea-Meadows upholstered furniture can be accomplished using its existing sales agents or with the Carrington sales force. Determining the most cost effective sales approach is one issue in the case.

How to Use the Worksheet

1.   Fill out the input form provided for this worksheet after reading the case you are analyzing.

2.   If you have not used any of the worksheets in this manual, please review the section of the manual on how to load Microsoft Excel or Lotus 1-2-3 for Windows, and the worksheets provided on the disk.

3.   Load the worksheet program. After the row and column format appears, load the worksheet using the keystrokes shown in the table below. See the section of the manual on how to load worksheets if you experience difficulties.

Keystrokes for Excel or 1-2-3W	Comments
[ALT] FO	Access the Command menu, the File menu and execute the Retrieve command.
CARFURN	Either type in the file name, or highlight the name using the cursor keys, or mouse.
[ENTER]	Press the Enter key to load the worksheet.

Table 17-1:   Load CARFURN worksheet

4.   After loading the worksheet, review it to make sure you know where the input cells are located. The input cells are colored differently than the rest of the cells on a color monitor. The first time you use the worksheet, most of the cells in the spreadsheet will display "NA", or "#NA", but don't worry. As you enter your input values, the NA's in the output cells will be replaced by calculated values.

Unless you have disabled the worksheet protection, only the input cells can be changed. If you accidentally attempt to change a protected (non-input) cell, the program will display an error message. Press the [ESC] key to return to normal operations.

The input sections of the worksheet for this case are boxed for emphasis in the figures below. Remember that the boxes do not show on the worksheet itself.

Worksheet

	A	B	C	D	E	F	G
1	Name = CarFurn						
2							
3	Input:			Carrington Furniture			
4	Commission rate as % paid to						
5	Lea-Meadows sales agents					#N/A	%
6	Commission rate as % paid to Carrington reps					#N/A	%
7	Current sales level in dollars					#N/A	
8	Amount paid to new sales reps					#N/A	
9	Current number of Lea-Meadow sales agents					#N/A	
10	Current number of Carrington sales reps					#N/A	
11	Average sales call time in hours					#N/A	Hours/call
12	Number of accounts					#N/A	Accts.
13	Average call frequency					#N/A	Calls/Acct.
14	Amount of available hours					#N/A	Hours
15							

5.   Type into the spreadsheet your estimates of the inputs using the information from the input forms you filled out in Step 1. Use the cursor keys ⬅, ➡, ⬇, and ⬆ to move to the desired cell location. Type in the number and press either the ENTER key or one of the cursor keys. Repeat this procedure until all the necessary input cells are filled.

Viewing the Spreadsheet Schedules and Graph

You can press the cursor keys (⬅, ➡, ⬇, and ⬆), or the Page Up PG↑ and the Page Down PG↓ keys to move around the worksheet area. Press the Home key to return to the upper left-hand corner of the spreadsheet.

The worksheet contains a graph. Click on the "Chart" tab to see the graph

Saving the Spreadsheet

After entering your estimates and examining the results, including the graph, save your spreadsheet by using the following commands.

Keystrokes for Excel or 1-2-3W	Comments
[ESC] [ESC]	If the top of the display screen shows one of the command menus, (see the introduction section of the manual) press the Escape key until the menus disappear. Skip this step if a menu is not displayed.
[ALT] FS	Access the Command menu, the File menu and the Save option.
[ENTER]	Press Enter to save under the same name. An Excel file is saved with a "XLS" suffix, and a 1-2-3 for Windows file is saved as a "WK4" file.

Table 17-2:   Save CARFURN worksheet

Printing the Worksheet

Place the mouse cursor on top of the "Print Worksheet" button to print it, and click on the "Print Chart" button to print the graph. Make sure you have a printer connected and turned on before attempting to print your results.

Bring the results of your analysis to class when the case is discussed.

Input Form for CARFURN

Name _____

Input: Carrington Furniture, Inc.

Commission rate as % paid to

   Lea-Meadows sales agents   _____%

Commission rate as % paid to Morgantown

       Furniture   _____%

Current sales level in dollars $_____

Amount paid to new sales reps   _____

Current number of Lea-Meadow sales agents   _____

Current number of Morgantown
      Furniture sales reps   _____

Average sales call time in hours   _____ Hours/call

Number of accounts   _____ Accts.

Average call frequency   _____ Calls/Acct.

Amount of available hours   _____ Hours

Output Form for CARFURN

Output:

Number of sales reps needed   _____ Reps

Incremental number of reps to hire   _____ Reps

Incremental Cost Comparison Cost for	Sales Agents	Sales Force
Commission	$_____	$_____
Salary	$_____	$_____
Totals	$_____	$_____

Chapter 18:
Cadbury Beverages, Inc.: CRUSH Brand

Introduction

Kim Feil was assigned the responsibility for managing the relaunch of the CRUSH soft drink brand for Cadbury Beverages Inc. Cadbury Beverages, Inc. had recently acquired the CRUSH, HIRES, and SUN-DROP soft drink brands from Procter & Gamble Company. Part of her task is determining the profitability of the CRUSH brand under different assumptions concerning the sales mix, selling price, and advertising and promotion expenditures.

How to Use the Worksheet

1.   Fill out the input form provided for this worksheet after reading the case you are analyzing.

2.   If you have not used any of the worksheets in this manual, please review the section of the manual on how to load Microsoft Excel or Lotus 1-2-3 for Windows, and the worksheets provided on the disk.

3.   Load the worksheet program. After the row and column format appears, load the worksheet using the keystrokes shown in the table below. See the section of the manual on how to load worksheets if you experience difficulties.

Keystrokes for Excel or 1-2-3W	Comments
[ALT] FO	Access the Command menu, the File menu and execute the Retrieve command.
CADBURY	Either type in the file name, or highlight the name using the cursor keys, or mouse.
[ENTER]	Press the Enter key to load the worksheet.

Table 18-1:   Load CADBURY worksheet

4.   After loading the worksheet, review it to make sure you know where the input cells are located. The input cells are colored differently than the rest of the cells on a color monitor. The first time you use the worksheet, most of the cells in the spreadsheet will display "NA", or "#NA", but don't worry. As you enter your input values, the NA's in the output cells will be replaced by calculated values.

Unless you have disabled the worksheet protection, only the input cells can be changed. If you accidentally attempt to change a protected (non-input) cell, the program will display an error message. Press the [ESC] key to return to normal operations.

The input sections of the worksheet for this case are boxed for emphasis in the figures below. Remember that the boxes do not show on the worksheet itself.

5.   Type into the spreadsheet your estimates of the inputs using the information from the input forms you filled out in Step 1. Use the cursor keys [↑], [↓], [←], and [→] to move to the

desired cell location. Type in the number and press either the [ENTER] key or one of the cursor keys. Repeat this procedure until all the necessary input cells are filled.

Worksheet

	A	B	C	D	E	F	G
1	Name = CADBURY						
2							
3	Cadbury Beverages Inc: Crush Brand						
4	Input:						
5		Regular		Diet		Both	
6	Sales mix percent	#N/A		#N/A			
7	Selling price/case	#N/A		#N/A			
8	Cost of goods sold/case	#N/A		#N/A			
9	Selling & Delivery per case					#N/A	
10	Adv. & Promotion:						
11	Media advertising (total $)					#N/A	
12	Promotion per case					#N/A	
13	General and Admin. Exp. per Case					#N/A	
14	Total units sold					#N/A	
15							

Viewing the Spreadsheet Schedules and Graph

You can press the cursor keys ([←], [→], [↓], and [↑]), or the Page Up [PG↑] and the Page Down [PG↓] keys to move around the worksheet area. Press the Home key to return to the upper left-hand corner of the spreadsheet.

The worksheet contains a graph. Click on the "Chart" tab to see the graph.

Saving the Spreadsheet

After entering your estimates and examining the results, including the graph, save your spreadsheet by using the following commands.

Keystrokes for Excel or 1-2-3W	Comments
[ESC] [ESC]	If the top of the display screen shows one of the command menus, (see the introduction section of the manual) press the Escape key until the menus disappear. Skip this step if a menu is not displayed.
[ALT] FS	Access the Command menu, the File menu and the Save option.
[ENTER]	Press Enter to save under the same name. An Excel file is saved with a "XLS" suffix, and a 1-2-3 for Windows file is saved as a "WK4" file.

Table 18-2:　Save COORS worksheet

Printing the Worksheet

Place the mouse cursor on top of the "Print Worksheet" button to print it, and click on the "Print Chart" button to print the graph. Make sure you have a printer connected and turned on before attempting to print your results.

Bring the results of your analysis to class when the case is discussed.

Input Form for CADBURY

Name _____

Cadbury Beverages Inc.: CRUSH Brand Pro Forma Income Statement

Input:	Regular	Diet	Both
Sales mix percent	_____	_____	
Selling price/case	$_____	$_____	
Cost of goods sold/case	$_____	$_____	
Selling & Delivery per case			$_____
Adv. & Promotion: Media advertising (total $)			$_____
Promotion per case			$_____
General and Admin. Exp. per Case			$_____
Total units sold			_____

Output Form for CADBURY

Name _____

Cadbury Beverages Inc: Crush Brand Pro Forma Income Statement

	Regular	%	Diet	%	Total	%
Net Sales:	$_____	__%	$_____	__%	$_____	100%
Cost of Goods Sold	$_____	__%	$_____	__%	$_____	__%
Gross Profit	$_____	__%	$_____	__%	$_____	__%
Selling and Delivery Exp.					$_____	__%
Advertising and Promotion Media Advertising					$_____	__%
Promotion					$_____	__%
General and Admin. Expense					$_____	__%
Total Expenses					$_____	__%
Pretax Cash Profit					$_____	__%

Chapter 19:
Southwest Airlines

Introduction

United Airlines introduced "Shuttle By United" service to compete with Southwest Airlines in California. After three months of head-to-head service, United announced that its shuttle service for the Oakland-Ontario market would be discontinued, and that all one-way walk up fares on shuttle flights would increase by $10. As a result, Southwest executives carefully examined the profitability of competing in other shuttle markets.

The spreadsheet allows you to select the cities for comparison using drop-down lists and to compare the estimated Southwest Airlines fourth quarter operating profits in Shuttle By United markets, with the Shuttle By United fourth quarter operating results. You enter the relevant items for each city pair.

How to Use the Worksheet

1.   Fill out the input form provided for this worksheet after reading the case you are analyzing.

2.   If you have not used any of the worksheets in this manual, please review the section of the manual on how to load Microsoft Excel or Lotus 1-2-3 for Windows, and the worksheets provided on the disk.

3.   Load the worksheet program. After the row and column format appears, load the worksheet using the keystrokes shown in the table below. See the section of the manual on how to load worksheets if you experience difficulties.

Keystrokes for Excel or 1-2-3W	Comments
[ALT] FO	Access the Command menu, the File menu and execute the Retrieve command.
SWAIR	Either type in the file name, or highlight the name using the cursor keys, or mouse.
[ENTER]	Press the Enter key to load the worksheet.

Table 19-1:   Load SWAIR worksheet

4.   After loading the worksheet, review it to make sure you know where the input cells are located. The input cells are colored differently than the rest of the cells on a color monitor. The first time you use the worksheet, most of the cells in the spreadsheet will display "NA", or "#NA", but don't worry. As you enter your input values, the NA's in the output cells will be replaced by calculated values.

Unless you have disabled the worksheet protection, only the input cells can be changed. If you accidentally attempt to change a protected (non-input) cell, the program will display an error message. Press the [ESC] key to return to normal operations.

The input sections of the worksheet for this case are boxed for emphasis in the figures below. Remember that the boxes do not show on the worksheet itself.

Worksheet

Name = SWAIR

Click on the buttons to select city pair for each row.

Estimated Southwest Airlines 1994 Fourth Quarter Operating Profits In Shuttle by United Competitive Markets

Market (City - Pair)		Avg. Fare	Air Miles	Route Yield	Load Factor %	Pass. Rev. per ASM	Cost per ASM	Op. Profit per ASM	Avail Seat Mi.	Daily Op. Profit
	▼	#N/A	#N/A		#N/A		#N/A		#N/A	
	▼	#N/A	#N/A		#N/A		#N/A		#N/A	
	▼	#N/A	#N/A		#N/A		#N/A		#N/A	
	▼	#N/A	#N/A		#N/A		#N/A		#N/A	
	▼	#N/A	#N/A		#N/A		#N/A		#N/A	
	▼	#N/A	#N/A		#N/A		#N/A		#N/A	
	▼	#N/A	#N/A		#N/A		#N/A		#N/A	
	▼	#N/A	#N/A		#N/A		#N/A		#N/A	
	▼	#N/A	#N/A		#N/A		#N/A		#N/A	
	▼	#N/A	#N/A		#N/A		#N/A		#N/A	
	▼									
	▼									
	▼									
	▼									
Total Daily Operating Profit										$ -

Shuttle By United: Estimated 1994 Fourth Quarter Operating Results

Market (City - Pair)		Avg. Fare	Air Miles	Route Yield	Load Factor %	Pass. Rev. per ASM	Cost per ASM	Op. Profit per ASM	Avail Seat Mi.	Daily Op. Profit
	▼	#N/A	#N/A		#N/A		#N/A		#N/A	
	▼	#N/A	#N/A		#N/A		#N/A		#N/A	
	▼	#N/A	#N/A		#N/A		#N/A		#N/A	
	▼	#N/A	#N/A		#N/A		#N/A		#N/A	
	▼	#N/A	#N/A		#N/A		#N/A		#N/A	
	▼	#N/A	#N/A		#N/A		#N/A		#N/A	
	▼	#N/A	#N/A		#N/A		#N/A		#N/A	
	▼	#N/A	#N/A		#N/A		#N/A		#N/A	
	▼	#N/A	#N/A		#N/A		#N/A		#N/A	
	▼	#N/A	#N/A		#N/A		#N/A		#N/A	
	▼	#N/A	#N/A		#N/A		#N/A		#N/A	
	▼	#N/A	#N/A		#N/A		#N/A		#N/A	
	▼									
Total Daily Operating Profit										$ -

5.   Type into the spreadsheet your estimates of the inputs using the information from the input forms you filled out in Step 1. Use the cursor keys ⬅, ➡, ⬇, and ⬆ to move to the desired cell location. Type in the number and press either the ENTER key or one of the cursor keys. Repeat this procedure until all the necessary input cells are filled.

Viewing the Spreadsheet Schedules and Graph

You can press the cursor keys (⬅, ➡, ⬇, and ⬆), or the Page Up PG↑ and the Page Down PG↓ keys to move around the worksheet area. Press the Home key to return to the upper left-hand corner of the spreadsheet.

The worksheet contains a graph. Click on the "Chart" tab to see the graph.

Saving the Spreadsheet

After entering your estimates and examining the results, including the graph, save your spreadsheet by using the following commands.

Keystrokes for Excel or 1-2-3W	Comments
ESC ESC	If the top of the display screen shows one of the command menus, (see the introduction section of the manual) press the Escape key until the menus disappear. Skip this step if a menu is not displayed.
ALT FS	Access the Command menu, the File menu and the Save option.
ENTER	Press Enter to save under the same name. An Excel file is saved with a "XLS" suffix, and a 1-2-3 for Windows file is saved as a "WK4" file.

Table 19-2:   Save SWAIR worksheet

Printing the Worksheet

Place the mouse cursor on top of the "Print Worksheet" button to print it, and click on the "Print Chart" button to print the graph. Make sure you have a printer connected and turned on before attempting to print your results.

Bring the results of your analysis to class when the case is discussed.

Input Form for SWAIR – Page 1 of 2

Name _____

Estimated Southwest Airlines 1994 Fourth Quarter Operating Profits In Shuttle by United Competitive Markets

Market City Pair	Avg. Fare	Air Miles	Load Factor%	Cost Per ASM	Avail. Seat Mi.
_____	_____	_____	_____	_____	_____
_____	_____	_____	_____	_____	_____
_____	_____	_____	_____	_____	_____
_____	_____	_____	_____	_____	_____
_____	_____	_____	_____	_____	_____
_____	_____	_____	_____	_____	_____
_____	_____	_____	_____	_____	_____
_____	_____	_____	_____	_____	_____
_____	_____	_____	_____	_____	_____
_____	_____	_____	_____	_____	_____
_____	_____	_____	_____	_____	_____
_____	_____	_____	_____	_____	_____
_____	_____	_____	_____	_____	_____

Input Form for SWAIR – Page 2 of 2

Shuttle By United: Estimated 1994 Fourth Quarter Operating Results

Market City Pair	Avg. Fare	Air Miles	Load Factor%	Cost Per ASM	Avail. Seat Mi.
_____	_____	_____	_____	_____	_____
_____	_____	_____	_____	_____	_____
_____	_____	_____	_____	_____	_____
_____	_____	_____	_____	_____	_____
_____	_____	_____	_____	_____	_____
_____	_____	_____	_____	_____	_____
_____	_____	_____	_____	_____	_____
_____	_____	_____	_____	_____	_____
_____	_____	_____	_____	_____	_____
_____	_____	_____	_____	_____	_____
_____	_____	_____	_____	_____	_____
_____	_____	_____	_____	_____	_____
_____	_____	_____	_____	_____	_____
_____	_____	_____	_____	_____	_____

Output Form for SWAIR– Page 1 of 2

Name _____

**Estimated Southwest Airlines 1994 Fourth Quarter Operating Profits
In Shuttle by United Competitive Markets**

Market (City - Pair)	Route Yield	Pass. Rev Per ASM	Costs Per ASM	Daily Op. Profit
_____	_____	_____	_____	_____
_____	_____	_____	_____	_____
_____	_____	_____	_____	_____
_____	_____	_____	_____	_____
_____	_____	_____	_____	_____
_____	_____	_____	_____	_____
_____	_____	_____	_____	_____
_____	_____	_____	_____	_____
_____	_____	_____	_____	_____
_____	_____	_____	_____	_____
_____	_____	_____	_____	_____
_____	_____	_____	_____	_____
_____	_____	_____	_____	_____

Total Daily Operating Profit   _____

Output Form for SWAIR– Page 2 of 2

Shuttle By United: Estimated 1994 Fourth Quarter Operating Results

Market (City - Pair)	Route Yield	Pass. Rev Per ASM	Costs Per ASM	Daily Op. Profit
_____	_____	_____	_____	_____
_____	_____	_____	_____	_____
_____	_____	_____	_____	_____
_____	_____	_____	_____	_____
_____	_____	_____	_____	_____
_____	_____	_____	_____	_____
_____	_____	_____	_____	_____
_____	_____	_____	_____	_____
_____	_____	_____	_____	_____
_____	_____	_____	_____	_____
_____	_____	_____	_____	_____
_____	_____	_____	_____	_____
_____	_____	_____	_____	_____

Total Daily Operating Profit   _____

Chapter 20:
Atlas Electronics Corporation

Introduction

Adrian Bartos, manager of facsimile technology engineering5 at Atlas Electronics, has just learned that a competitor had underbid the company on an order for its digital converter semiconductor device for facsimile machines. He is confident that the competitor's bid price was unrealistically low since Atlas could only meet the bid only by pricing with significantly lower profit margins. He assembled his staff and to formulate a course of action to take concerning the bid price and to examine his product's unit costs using a learning curve.

How to Use the Worksheet

1.   Fill out the input form provided for this worksheet after reading the case you are analyzing.

2.   If you have not used any of the worksheets in this manual, please review the section of the manual on how to load Microsoft Excel or Lotus 1-2-3 for Windows, and the worksheets provided on the disk.

3.   Load the worksheet program. After the row and column format appears, load the worksheet using the keystrokes shown in the table below. See the section of the manual on how to load worksheets if you experience difficulties.

Keystrokes for Excel or 1-2-3W	Comments
[ALT] FO	Access the Command menu, the File menu and execute the Retrieve command.
ATLAS	Either type in the file name, or highlight the name using the cursor keys, or mouse.
[ENTER]	Press the Enter key to load the worksheet.

Table 20-1:   Load ATLAS worksheet

4.   After loading the worksheet, review it to make sure you know where the input cells are located. The input cells are colored differently than the rest of the cells on a color monitor. The first time you use the worksheet, most of the cells in the spreadsheet will display "NA", or "#NA", but don't worry. As you enter your input values, the NA's in the output cells will be replaced by calculated values.

Unless you have disabled the worksheet protection, only the input cells can be changed. If you accidentally attempt to change a protected (non-input) cell, the program will display an error message. Press the [ESC] key to return to normal operations.

The input sections of the worksheet for this case are boxed for emphasis in the figures below. Remember that the boxes do not show on the worksheet itself.

Worksheet

	A	B	C	D	E	F
1	Name = ATLAS					
2						
3	Atlas Electronics				Input	
4	Learning Curve Rate as a percent				#N/A	
5	Cumulative average time required for lot				#N/A	
6	Number of units in each lot				#N/A	
7	Material cost per unit				#N/A	
8	Labor rate per hour				#N/A	
9	Quoted sales price				#N/A	

5.   Type into the spreadsheet your estimates of the inputs using the information from the input forms you filled out in Step 1. Use the cursor keys ⬅, ➡, ⬇, and ⬆ to move to the desired cell location. Type in the number and press either the ⏎ENTER key or one of the cursor keys. Repeat this procedure until all the necessary input cells are filled.

Viewing the Spreadsheet Schedules and Graph

You can press the cursor keys (⬅, ➡, ⬇, and ⬆), or the Page Up [PG↑] and the Page Down [PG↓] keys to move around the worksheet area. Press the Home key to return to the upper left-hand corner of the spreadsheet.

The worksheet contains a graph. Click on the "Chart" tab to see the graph.

Saving the Spreadsheet

After entering your estimates and examining the results, including the graph, save your spreadsheet by using the following commands.

Keystrokes for Excel or 1-2-3W	Comments
[ESC] [ESC]	If the top of the display screen shows one of the command menus, (see the introduction section of the manual) press the Escape key until the menus disappear. Skip this step if a menu is not displayed.
[ALT] FS	Access the Command menu, the File menu and the Save option.
[ENTER]	Press Enter to save under the same name. An Excel file is saved with a "XLS" suffix, and a 1-2-3 for Windows file is saved as a "WK4" file.

Table 20-2:   Save ATLAS worksheet

Printing the Worksheet

Place the mouse cursor on top of the "Print Worksheet" button to print it, and click on the "Print Chart" button to print the graph. Make sure you have a printer connected and turned on before attempting to print your results.

Bring the results of your analysis to class when the case is discussed.

Input Form for ATLAS

Atlas Electronics Corporation: Facsimile Technology Program

	Input	
Learning Curve Rate as a percent	_____	%
Cumulative average time required for lot	_____	hours
Number of units in each lot	_____	unit/lot
Material cost per unit	$_____	$/unit
Labor rate per hour	$_____	$/hour
Quoted sales price	$_____	per unit

Output Form for ATLAS -- Part 1 of 2

Name _____

Units	Average DL Hours	Total Labor $	Total Mat. $	Total Cost	Avg. Cost Per Unit
_____	_____	$_____	$_____	$_____	$_____
_____	_____	$_____	$_____	$_____	$_____
_____	_____	$_____	$_____	$_____	$_____
_____	_____	$_____	$_____	$_____	$_____
_____	_____	$_____	$_____	$_____	$_____
_____	_____	$_____	$_____	$_____	$_____
_____	_____	$_____	$_____	$_____	$_____
_____	_____	$_____	$_____	$_____	$_____

Output Form for ATLAS -- Part 1 of 2

Cumulative Revenue, Cost, and Income Summary

Units	Revenue	Costs	Income	Income as % of sales
_____	$_____	$_____	$_____	_____%
_____	$_____	$_____	$_____	_____%
_____	$_____	$_____	$_____	_____%
_____	$_____	$_____	$_____	_____%
_____	$_____	$_____	$_____	_____%
_____	$_____	$_____	$_____	_____%
_____	$_____	$_____	$_____	_____%
_____	$_____	$_____	$_____	_____%

Chapter 21:
Augustine Medical, Inc.: Bair Hugger

Introduction

In early 1988, executives at Augustine Medical, Inc. had to determine how to price The Bair Hugger Patient Warming System. Pricing this system is made complex by the fact that two components of the system must be priced: (1) a heater/blower unit and (2) warming covers or blankets. Company executives must determine a list price for the heater/blower unit and warming covers and assess the profit potential of The Bair Hugger Patient Warming System.

How to Use the Worksheet

1. Fill out the input form provided for this worksheet after reading the case you are analyzing.

2. If you have not used any of the worksheets in this manual, please review the section of the manual on how to load Microsoft Excel or Lotus 1-2-3 for Windows, and the worksheets provided on the disk.

3. Load the worksheet program. After the row and column format appears, load the worksheet using the keystrokes shown in the table below. See the section of the manual on how to load worksheets if you experience difficulties.

Keystrokes for Excel or 1-2-3W	Comments
[ALT] FO	Access the Command menu, the File menu and execute the Retrieve command.
AUGUST	Either type in the file name, or highlight the name using the cursor keys, or mouse.
[ENTER]	Press the Enter key to load the worksheet.

Table 21-1:   Load AUGUST worksheet

4. After loading the worksheet, review it to make sure you know where the input cells are located. The input cells are colored differently than the rest of the cells on a color monitor. The first time you use the worksheet, most of the cells in the spreadsheet will display "NA", or "#NA", but don't worry. As you enter your input values, the NA's in the output cells will be replaced by calculated values.

Unless you have disabled the worksheet protection, only the input cells can be changed. If you accidentally attempt to change a protected (non-input) cell, the program will display an error message. Press the [ESC] key to return to normal operations.

The input sections of the worksheet for this case are boxed for emphasis in the figures below. Remember that the boxes do not show on the worksheet itself.

Worksheet

	A	B	C	D	E	F	G
1	Name = AUGUST						
2							
3				Augustine Medical, Inc.			
4				The Bair Hugger Patient Warming System			
5							
6	INPUTS:						
7						Heater	
8						Blower Unit	Blankets
9	Enter Beginning Price per unit					#N/A	#N/A
10	Enter discount for						
11	manufacturers price as						
12	a percent					#N/A	#N/A
13	Enter interval for						
14	Price Schedule					#N/A	#N/A
15	Number of Blankets Sold per						
16	Heater/Blower Installation						#N/A
17	Direct Cost					#N/A	#N/A
18	Total Fixed Cost Required						
19	for Project						#N/A
20	Desired Return on Investment						
21	(enter as a percent)						#N/A

5.   Type into the spreadsheet your estimates of the inputs using the information from the input forms you filled out in Step 1. Use the cursor keys ⬅, ➡, ⬇, and ⬆ to move to the desired cell location. Type in the number and press either the [ENTER] key or one of the cursor keys. Repeat this procedure until all the necessary input cells are filled.

Viewing the Spreadsheet Schedules and Graph

You can press the cursor keys (⬅, ➡, ⬇, and ⬆), or the Page Up [PG↑] and the Page Down [PG↓] keys to move around the worksheet area. Press the Home key to return to the upper left-hand corner of the spreadsheet.

The worksheet contains a graph. Click on the "Chart" tab to see the graph.

Saving the Spreadsheet

After entering your estimates and examining the results, including the graph, save your spreadsheet by using the following commands.

Keystrokes for Excel or 1-2-3W	Comments
[ESC] [ESC]	If the top of the display screen shows one of the command menus, (see the introduction section of the manual) press the Escape key until the menus disappear. Skip this step if a menu is not displayed.
[ALT] FS	Access the Command menu, the File menu and the Save option.
[ENTER]	Press Enter to save under the same name. An Excel file is saved with a "XLS" suffix, and a 1-2-3 for Windows file is saved as a "WK4" file.

Table 21-2:   Save AUGUST worksheet

Printing the Worksheet

Place the mouse cursor on top of the "Print Worksheet" button to print it, and click on the "Print Chart" button to print the graph. Make sure you have a printer connected and turned on before attempting to print your results.

Bring the results of your analysis to class when the case is discussed.

Input Form for AUGUST - First Analysis

Name _____

Augustine Medical, Inc.
The Bair Hugger Patient Warming System

INPUT FORM	Heater Blower Unit	Blankets
Enter Beginning Price per unit	_____	_____
Enter discount for manufacturer's price as a percent	_____	_____
Enter interval for Price Schedule	_____	_____
Number of Blankets Sold per Heater/Blower Installation		_____
Direct Cost	_____	_____
Total Fixed Cost Required for Project		_____
Desired Return on Investment (enter as a percent)		_____

Output Form for AUGUST - First Analysis

Name _____

Break Even Report

	Price Range	
	Low Value	High Value
Range of prices for unit calculations :		
Heater/Blower Full Retail Price	_____	_____
Blanket Full Retail Price	_____	_____

For the above price ranges the
following values are
calculated:

	Price Range	
	Low Value	High Value
Contribution in Dollars for low and high system unit combinations.	_____	_____

Break Even Points in
units sold for low and high
contribution combinations.

	Low Value	High Value
System Units	_____	_____
Blower Units	_____	_____
Blankets	_____	_____

Volume in units required to earn
specified ROI at low and high
contribution combinations.

	Low Value	High Value
System Units	_____	_____
Blower Units	_____	_____
Blankets	_____	_____

Augustine Medical, Inc.

Input Form for AUGUST - Second Analysis

Name _____

Augustine Medical, Inc.
The Bair Hugger Patient Warming System

INPUT FORM	Heater Blower Unit	Blankets
Enter Beginning Price per unit	_____	_____
Enter discount for manufacturers price as a percent	_____	_____
Enter interval for Price Schedule	_____	_____
Number of Blankets Sold per Heater/Blower Installation		_____
Direct Cost	_____	_____
Total Fixed Cost Required for Project		_____
Desired Return on Investment (enter as a percent)		_____

Output Form for AUGUST - Second Analysis

Name _____

                              Break Even Report

                                   Price Range
Range of prices for unit   Low Value   High Value
calculations :
Heater/Blower Full Retail Price   _____ _____

Blanket Full Retail Price   _____ _____

For the above price ranges the
following values are
calculated: Price Range
                                  Low Value   High Value
Contribution in Dollars for
 low and high system unit
 combinations.   _____ _____

Break Even Points in
 units sold for low and high   Low Value   High Value
 contribution combinations.
         System Units   _____ _____

         Blower Units   _____ _____

         Blankets   _____ _____

Volume in units required to earn
 specified ROI at low and high   Low Value   High Value
 contribution combinations.
         System Units   _____ _____

         Blower Units   _____ _____

         Blankets   _____ _____

Chapter 22:
North Pittsburgh Telephone Company

Introduction

In late 1992, Greg Sloan, marketing supervisor of the North Pittsburgh Telephone Company was considering whether or not to employ usage-sensitive pricing for a forthcoming introduction of new telephone services called CLASS services. The company is introducing CLASS service on January 1, 1993. Greg Sloan has several options to consider concerning pricing for the service. The spreadsheet helps with the analysis of the different pricing strategies.

How to Use the Worksheet

1.   Fill out the input form provided for this worksheet after reading the case you are analyzing.

2.   If you have not used any of the worksheets in this manual, please review the section of the manual on how to load Microsoft Excel or Lotus 1-2-3 for Windows, and the worksheets provided on the disk.

3.   Load the worksheet program. After the row and column format appears, load the worksheet using the keystrokes shown in the table below. See the section of the manual on how to load worksheets if you experience difficulties.

Keystrokes for Excel or 1-2-3W	Comments
[ALT] FO	Access the Command menu, the File menu and execute the Retrieve command.
NORPITT	Either type in the file name, or highlight the name using the cursor keys, or mouse.
[ENTER]	Press the Enter key to load the worksheet.

Table 22-1:   Load NORPITT worksheet

4.   After loading the worksheet, review it to make sure you know where the input cells are located. The input cells are colored differently than the rest of the cells on a color monitor. The first time you use the worksheet, most of the cells in the spreadsheet will display "NA", or "#NA", but don't worry. As you enter your input values, the NA's in the output cells will be replaced by calculated values.

Unless you have disabled the worksheet protection, only the input cells can be changed. If you accidentally attempt to change a protected (non-input) cell, the program will display an error message. Press the [ESC] key to return to normal operations.

The input sections of the worksheet for this case are boxed for emphasis in the figures below. Remember that the boxes do not show on the worksheet itself.

Worksheet

	A	B	C	D	E	F	G	H
1	Name = NorPitt							
2								
3	Inputs:							
4	Number of service lines in 1992					#N/A		
5	Annual average growth rate for service lines					#N/A	%	
6								
7	Schedules:							
8	Monthly subscription price annual revenue projections							
9	based on Northern Telecom Penetration Rates and Average Price							
10	Points for Class Services							
11	Year	Estimated Penetration (%)	Service Lines	Annual Revenue Projections at Average Monthly Price Points				
12				$ 3.25	$ 3.50	$ 3.75		
13	1993	#N/A	#N/A	#N/A	#N/A	#N/A		
14	1994	#N/A	#N/A	#N/A	#N/A	#N/A		
15	1995	#N/A	#N/A	#N/A	#N/A	#N/A		
16	1996	#N/A	#N/A	#N/A	#N/A	#N/A		
17	1997	#N/A	#N/A	#N/A	#N/A	#N/A		
18	Total Revenue			#N/A	#N/A	#N/A		
19								
20								
21	Annual Revenue Projections Based on Northern Telecom Penetration Rates							
22	and Activation Rates at Different Usage Rates							
23	Year	Estimated Penetration (%)	Service Lines	Monthly Activations	Activation Rates per Use:			
24					$ 0.25	$ 0.50	$ 0.75	$ 1.00
25	1993	#N/A	#N/A	#N/A	#N/A	#N/A	#N/A	#N/A
26	1994	#N/A	#N/A	#N/A	#N/A	#N/A	#N/A	#N/A
27	1995	#N/A	#N/A	#N/A	#N/A	#N/A	#N/A	#N/A
28	1996	#N/A	#N/A	#N/A	#N/A	#N/A	#N/A	#N/A
29	1997	#N/A	#N/A	#N/A	#N/A	#N/A	#N/A	#N/A
30	Total Revenue				#N/A	#N/A	#N/A	#N/A

5.   Type into the spreadsheet your estimates of the inputs using the information from the input forms you filled out in Step 1. Use the cursor keys ⬅, ➡, ⬇, and ⬆ to move to the desired cell location. Type in the number and press either the [ENTER] key or one of the cursor keys. Repeat this procedure until all the necessary input cells are filled.

Viewing the Spreadsheet Schedules and Graph

You can press the cursor keys (⬅, ➡, ⬇, and ⬆), or the Page Up [PG↑] and the Page Down [PG↓] keys to move around the worksheet area. Press the Home key to return to the upper left-hand corner of the spreadsheet.

The worksheet contains a graph. Click on the "Chart" tab to see the graph.

Saving the Spreadsheet

After entering your estimates and examining the results, including the graph, save your spreadsheet by using the following commands.

Keystrokes for Excel or 1-2-3W	Comments
[ESC] [ESC]	If the top of the display screen shows one of the command menus, (see the introduction section of the manual) press the Escape key until the menus disappear. Skip this step if a menu is not displayed.
[ALT] FS	Access the Command menu, the File menu and the Save option.
[ENTER]	Press Enter to save under the same name. An Excel file is saved with a "XLS" suffix, and a 1-2-3 for Windows file is saved as a "WK4" file.

Table 22-2:   Save NORPITT worksheet

Printing the Worksheet

Place the mouse cursor on top of the "Print Worksheet" button to print it, and click on the "Print Chart" button to print the graph. Make sure you have a printer connected and turned on before attempting to print your results.

Bring the results of your analysis to class when the case is discussed.

Input Form for NORPITT

Name _____

Number of service lines in 1992   _____

Annual average growth rate for service lines   _____

Monthly subscription price annual revenue projections
based on Northern Telecom Penetration Rates and Average Price Points for Class Services

Year   Estimated Penetration (%)

1993   _____

1994   _____

1995   _____

1996   _____

1997   _____

Annual Revenue Projections Based on Northern Telecom Penetration Rates and Activation
Rates at Different Usage Rates
Year   Estimated Penetration (%)   Monthly Activations

1993   _____   _____

1994   _____   _____

1995   _____   _____

1996   _____   _____

1997   _____   _____

Output Form for NORPITT

Name _____

Monthly subscription price annual revenue projections based on Northern Telecom
Penetration Rates and Average Price Points for Class Services

Year	Est. Penet %	Service Lines	Monthly Price Points $_____	$_____	$_____
1993	_____	_____	_____	_____	_____
1994	_____	_____	_____	_____	_____
1995	_____	_____	_____	_____	_____
1996	_____	_____	_____	_____	_____
1997	_____	_____	_____	_____	_____
Total Revenue			_____	_____	_____

Annual Revenue Projections Based on Northern Telecom Penetration Rates and Activation
Rates at Different Usage Rates

Year	Est. Penet. %	Service Lines	Monthly Activations.
1993	_____	_____	_____
1994	_____	_____	_____
1995	_____	_____	_____
1996	_____	_____	_____
1997	_____	_____	_____
Total Revenue		_____	

Activation Rates per Use: $_____ $_____ $_____ $_____

Year				
1993	_____	_____	_____	_____
1994	_____	_____	_____	_____
1995	_____	_____	_____	_____
1996	_____	_____	_____	_____
1997	_____	_____	_____	_____
Total Revenue	_____	_____	_____	_____

Chapter 23:
The Circle K Corporation

Introduction

The Circle K Corporation filed for protection under Chapter 11 of the United States Bankruptcy code. A short time later, the Circle K president Robert A. Dearth, Jr. announced that he was planning a turnaround strategy for implementation in the summer of 1990. Part of this strategy requires changes in merchandising practices, increased promotional efforts, store closings and an aggressive pricing program. These changes should increase sales and improve customer service, and reduce costs.

How to Use the Worksheet

1.   Fill out the input form provided for this worksheet after reading the case you are analyzing.

2.   If you have not used any of the worksheets in this manual, please review the section of the manual on how to load Microsoft Excel or Lotus 1-2-3 for Windows, and the worksheets provided on the disk.

3.   Load the worksheet program. After the row and column format appears, load the worksheet using the keystrokes shown in the table below. See the section of the manual on how to load worksheets if you experience difficulties.

Keystrokes for Excel or 1-2-3W	Comments
[ALT] FO	Access the Command menu, the File menu and execute the Retrieve command.
CIRCLE	Either type in the file name, or highlight the name using the cursor keys, or mouse.
[ENTER]	Press the Enter key to load the worksheet.

Table 23-1:   Load CIRCLE worksheet

4.   After loading the worksheet, review it to make sure you know where the input cells are located. The input cells are colored differently than the rest of the cells on a color monitor. The first time you use the worksheet, most of the cells in the spreadsheet will display "NA", or "#NA", but don't worry. As you enter your input values, the NA's in the output cells will be replaced by calculated values.

Unless you have disabled the worksheet protection, only the input cells can be changed. If you accidentally attempt to change a protected (non-input) cell, the program will display an error message. Press the [ESC] key to return to normal operations.

The input sections of the worksheet for this case are boxed for emphasis in the figures below. Remember that the boxes do not show on the worksheet itself.

Worksheet

	A	B	C	D	E
1	Name = CIRCLE				
2	Revenue and Expense Worksheet for Circle K's Announced Turnaround Strategy				
3					Fiscal 1991
4		Fiscal 1990	Percent		Projection
5		Figure ($000)	Change		($000)
6	A. Sales volume change:				
7	Due to price decrease (includes				
8	merchandise and gasoline)	$3,686,314	#N/A	%	#N/A
9	Due to merchandise policy (omits				
10	gasoline sales)	$1,869,400	#N/A	%	#N/A
11	Due to advertising/promotion				
12	(includes merchandise and				
13	gasoline)	$3,686,314	#N/A	%	#N/A
14	Due to closed stores (includes				
15	merchandise and gasoline)	$3,686,314	#N/A	%	#N/A
16	B. Incremental change in sales				#N/A
17	C. Base: fiscal 1990 sales				$3,686,314
18	D. Projected fiscal 1990 sales				#N/A
19	E. Estimated percentage sales increase for 1991				#N/A
20	F. Projected gross profit percent in 1991		#N/A	%	
21	G. Projected fiscal 1991 gross profit in dollars				#N/A
22	H. Expense change:				
23	Operating and administrative	$865,602	#N/A	%	#N/A
24	Depreciation and amortization	$127,652	#N/A	%	#N/A
25	I. Projected expenses				#N/A
26	J. Projected operating profit				#N/A
27					

5.   Type into the spreadsheet your estimates of the inputs using the information from the input forms you filled out in Step 1. Use the cursor keys ⬅, ➡, ⬇, and ⬆ to move to the desired cell location. Type in the number and press either the ⌨ENTER⌨ key or one of the cursor keys. Repeat this procedure until all the necessary input cells are filled.

Viewing the Spreadsheet Schedules and Graph

You can press the cursor keys (⬅, ➡, ⬇, and ⬆), or the Page Up ⌨PG↑⌨ and the Page Down ⌨PG↓⌨ keys to move around the worksheet area. Press the Home key to return to the upper left-hand corner of the spreadsheet.

The worksheet contains a graph. Click on the "Chart" tab to see the graph.

Saving the Spreadsheet

After entering your estimates and examining the results, including the graph, save your spreadsheet by using the following commands.

Keystrokes for Excel or 1-2-3W	Comments
[ESC] [ESC]	If the top of the display screen shows one of the command menus, (see the introduction section of the manual) press the Escape key until the menus disappear. Skip this step if a menu is not displayed.
[ALT] FS	Access the Command menu, the File menu and the Save option.
[ENTER]	Press Enter to save under the same name. An Excel file is saved with a "XLS" suffix, and a 1-2-3 for Windows file is saved as a "WK4" file.

Table 23-2:   Save CIRCLE worksheet

Printing the Worksheet

Place the mouse cursor on top of the "Print Worksheet" button to print it, and click on the "Print Chart" button to print the graph. Make sure you have a printer connected and turned on before attempting to print your results.

Bring the results of your analysis to class when the case is discussed.

Input Form for CIRCLE

Name _____

Sales volume change due to:
  Price decrease   _____

  Merchandise policy   _____

  Closed stores   _____

Estimated gross profit percent   _____

Expense change in:
  Operating and admin. expense   _____

  Depreciation and amortization   _____

Output Form for CIRCLE

Revenue and Expense Worksheet for Circle K's Turnaround Strategy

	Fiscal 1990 Figure ($000)	Percent Change	Fiscal 1991 ($000)
A. Sales volume change:			
Due to price decrease (includes merchandise and gasoline)	$3,686,314	_____ %	$_____
Due to merchandise Policy (omits gasoline sales)	$1,869,400	_____ %	$_____
Due to advertising/promotion (includes merchandise and gasoline)	$3,686,314	_____ %	$_____
Due to closed stores (includes merchandise and gasoline)	$3,686,314	_____ %	$_____
B. Incremental change in sales			$_____
C. Base: fiscal 1990 sales			$_____
D. Projected fiscal 1990 sales			$_____
E. Estimated percentage sales increase for 1991			_____ %
F. Projected gross profit percent in 1991		_____ %	
G. Projected fiscal 1991 gross profit in dollars			$_____
H. Expense change:			
Operating and administrative	$865,602	_____ %	$_____
Depreciation and amortization	$127,652	_____ %	$_____
I. Projected expenses			$_____
J. Projected operating profit			$_____

Chapter 24:
Macon Institutue of Art and History

Introduction

In early 1996, Ashley Mercer, Directory of Development and Community Affairs, and Donald Pate, Director of Finance and Administration of the Macon Institute of Art and History met to discuss events occurring in a meeting the previous day. During the meeting the senior staff and members of the Institute's Board of Trustees had closely examined the financial status of the Institute because it had just incurred its third consecutive year of losses and museum reserves were depleted.. Ashley Mercer and Donald Pate were assigned the responsibility for making recommendations that would improve the Institute's financial position.

How to Use the Worksheet

1.   Fill out the input form provided for this worksheet after reading the case you are analyzing.

2.   If you have not used any of the worksheets in this manual, please review the section of the manual on how to load Microsoft Excel or Lotus 1-2-3 for Windows, and the worksheets provided on the disk.

3.   Load the worksheet program. After the row and column format appears, load the worksheet using the keystrokes shown in the table below. See the section of the manual on how to load worksheets if you experience difficulties.

Keystrokes for Excel or 1-2-3W	Comments
ALT FO	Access the Command menu, the File menu and execute the Retrieve command.
MACON	Either type in the file name, or highlight the name using the cursor keys, or mouse.
ENTER	Press the Enter key to load the worksheet.
Table 24-1: Load MACON worksheet	

4.   After loading the worksheet, review it to make sure you know where the input cells are located. The input cells are colored differently than the rest of the cells on a color monitor. The first time you use the worksheet, most of the cells in the spreadsheet will display "NA", or "#NA", but don't worry. As you enter your input values, the NA's in the output cells will be replaced by calculated values.

Unless you have disabled the worksheet protection, only the input cells can be changed. If you accidentally attempt to change a protected (non-input) cell, the program will display an error message. Press the ESC key to return to normal operations.

The input sections of the worksheet for this case are boxed for emphasis in the figures below. Remember that the boxes do not show on the worksheet itself.

Worksheet

	A	B	C	D	E
1	Name = MACON				
2					
3					
4	Macon Institure of Art and History Income and Expense Worksheet				
5					
6	OPERATIONS:	1996		1997	
7	INCOME:				
8	Appropriations - Fannel County	$1,786,929	26.84%	#N/A	#N/A
9	Contributions	338,664	5.09%	#N/A	#N/A
10	Grants	763,581	11.47%	#N/A	#N/A
11	Investment Income	27,878	0.42%	#N/A	#N/A
12	Earnings from Endowment	673,805	10.12%	#N/A	#N/A
13	Other	149,462	2.24%	#N/A	#N/A
14	Memberships	2,917,325	43.82%	#N/A	#N/A
15	Total Revenue	$6,657,644	100.00%	#N/A	#N/A
16	EXPENSES:				
17	Personnel.	$1,973,218	29.64%	#N/A	#N/A
18	Publications/Public Information	594,067	8.92%	#N/A	#N/A
19	Education	616,828	9.26%	#N/A	#N/A
20	Administration	3,777,042	56.73%	#N/A	#N/A
21	Memberships	854,461	12.83%	#N/A	#N/A
22	Total Expenses	$7,815,616	117.39%	#N/A	#N/A
23	Operating Income	($1,157,972)	-17.39%	#N/A	#N/A
24	AUXILIARY-ACTIVITIES:				
25	Revenue from Auxiliary:				
26	Special Exhibitions	$1,655,200	39.07%	#N/A	#N/A
27	Institute Gift Shop	1,596,775	37.69%	#N/A	#N/A
28	Skyline Buffet	515,843	12.18%	#N/A	#N/A
29	Institute Parking	131,512	3.10%	#N/A	#N/A
30	Institute Association	337,136	7.96%	#N/A	#N/A
31	Total Revenue from Auxiliary	$4,236,466	100.00%	#N/A	#N/A
32	Expenses from Auxiliary:				
33	Special Exhibitions	$814,741	19.23%	#N/A	#N/A
34	Institute Gift Shop	1,679,294	39.64%	#N/A	#N/A
35	Skyline Buffet	592,051	13.98%	#N/A	#N/A
36	Institute Parking	31,168	0.74%	#N/A	#N/A
37	Institute Association	344,955	8.14%	#N/A	#N/A
38	Total Expenses from Auxiliary	$3,462,209	81.72%	#N/A	#N/A
39	PROFIT FROM AUXILIARY ACTIVITIES	$774,257	18.28%	#N/A	#N/A
40	NET INCOME-OPERATIONS AND				
41	AUXILIARY ACTIVITIES	($383,715)	-3.52%	#N/A	#N/A
42					

5.   Type into the spreadsheet your estimates of the inputs using the information from the input forms you filled out in Step 1. Use the cursor keys ⬅, ➡, ⬇, and ⬆ to move to the desired cell location. Type in the number and press either the ENTER key or one of the cursor keys. Repeat this procedure until all the necessary input cells are filled.

Viewing the Spreadsheet Schedules and Graph

You can press the cursor keys (⬅, ➡, ⬇, and ⬆), or the Page Up [PG↑] and the Page Down [PG↓] keys to move around the worksheet area. Press the Home key to return to the upper left-hand corner of the spreadsheet.

The worksheet contains a graph. Click on the "Chart" tab to see the graph.

Saving the Spreadsheet

After entering your estimates and examining the results, including the graph, save your spreadsheet by using the following commands.

Keystrokes for Excel or 1-2-3W	Comments
[ESC] [ESC]	If the top of the display screen shows one of the command menus, (see the introduction section of the manual) press the Escape key until the menus disappear. Skip this step if a menu is not displayed.
[ALT] FS	Access the Command menu, the File menu and the Save option.
[ENTER]	Press Enter to save under the same name. An Excel file is saved with a "XLS" suffix, and a 1-2-3 for Windows file is saved as a "WK4" file.

Table 24-2:   Save MACON worksheet

Printing the Worksheet

Place the mouse cursor on top of the "Print Worksheet" button to print it, and click on the "Print Chart" button to print the graph. Make sure you have a printer connected and turned on before attempting to print your results.

Bring the results of your analysis to class when the case is discussed.

Input Form for MACON

Macon Institute Art and History Income and Expense Worksheet

INCOME: 1996   1997

Appropriations - Fannel County $1,786,929 26.84% $_____

Contributions   338,664   5.09% $_____

Grants   763,581 11.47% $_____

Earnings from Endowment   673,805 10.12% $_____

Other   149,462   2.24% $_____

Memberships   2,917,325 43.82% $_____

EXPENSES:
Personnel $1,973,218 29.64% $_____

Publications/Public Information   594,067   8.92% $_____

Education   616,828   9.26% $_____

Administration   3,777,042 56.73% $_____

Revenue from Auxiliary:
  Special Exhibitions $1,655,200 39.07% $_____

  Institute Gift Shop   1,596,775 37.69% $_____

  Skyline Buffet   515,843 12.18% $_____

  Institute Parking   131,512   3.10% $_____

  Institute Association   337,136   7.96% $_____

Expenses from Auxiliary:
  Special Exhibitions $814,741 19.23% $_____

  Institute Gift Shop   1,679,294 39.64% $_____

  Skyline Buffet   592,051 13.98% $_____

  Institute Parking   31,168   0.74% $_____

  Institute Association   344,955   8.14% $_____

Output Form for MACON -- Part 1 of 2

Name _____

Macon Institute of Art and History
Income and Expense Worksheet

OPERATIONS:	1996	%	1997	%
INCOME:				
Appropriations - Fannel County	$1,786,929	26.84%	$_____	____%
Contributions	338,664	5.09%	$_____	____%
Grants	763,581	11.47%	$_____	____%
Investment Income	27,878	0.42%	$_____	____%
Earnings from Endowment	673,805	10.12%	$_____	____%
Other	149,462	2.24%	$_____	____%
Memberships	2,917,325	43.82%	$_____	____%
Total Revenue	$6,657,644	100.00%	$_____	____%
EXPENSES:				
Personnel	$1,973,218	29.64%	$_____	____%
Publications/Public Information	594,067	8.92%	$_____	____%
Education	616,828	9.26%	$_____	____%
Administration	3,777,042	56.73%	$_____	____%
Memberships	854,461	12.83%	$_____	____%
Total Expenses	$7,815,616	117.39%	$_____	____%
Operating Income	($1,157,972)	-17.39%	$_____	____%

Output Form for MACON Part 2 of 2

```
AUXILIARY-ACTIVITIES:
Revenue from Auxiliary:
  Special Exhibitions         $1,655,200  39.07%  $_____  ____%

  Institute Gift Shop          1,596,775  37.69%  $_____  ____%

  Skyline Buffet                 515,843  12.18%  $_____  ____%

  Institute Parking              131,512   3.10%  $_____  ____%

  Institute Association          337,136   7.96%  $_____  ____%

  Total Revenue from Auxiliary $4,236,466 100.00% $_____  ____%

Expenses from Auxiliary:
  Special Exhibitions           $814,741  19.23%  $_____  ____%

  Institute Gift Shop          1,679,294  39.64%  $_____  ____%

  Skyline Buffet                 592,051  13.98%  $_____  ____%

  Institute Parking               31,168   0.74%  $_____  ____%

  Institute Association          344,955   8.14%  $_____  ____%

 Total Expenses from Auxiliary $3,462,209 81.72%  $_____  ____%

PROFIT FROM AUXILIARY ACTIVITIES $774,257 18.28%  $_____  ____%

NET INCOME-OPERATIONS AND
  AUXILIARY ACTIVITIES         ($383,715) -3.52%  $_____  ____%
```

Chapter 25:
Show Circuit Frozen Dog Dinner

Introduction

Food brokers had approached Tyler Pet Foods about the possibility of entering the household dog food market in Boston with their "Show Circuit Dog Dinner." They had heard of a similar product being sold in selected pet stores in the southwestern United States and believed that a great potential existed in selling Show Circuit through supermarkets. The company hired a consulting firm to develop a market entry program for introducing the product on a limited basis through supermarkets to the household dog food market in the Boston metropolitan area. The company must decide to accept, reject, or modify the proposed introductory marketing program.

How to Use the Worksheet

1.   Fill out the input form provided for this worksheet after reading the case you are analyzing.

2.   If you have not used any of the worksheets in this manual, please review the section of the manual on how to load Microsoft Excel or Lotus 1-2-3 for Windows, and the worksheets provided on the disk.

3.   Load the worksheet program. After the row and column format appears, load the worksheet using the keystrokes shown in the table below. See the section of the manual on how to load worksheets if you experience difficulties.

Keystrokes for Excel or 1-2-3W	Comments
[ALT] FO	Access the Command menu, the File menu and execute the Retrieve command.
SHOW	Either type in the file name, or highlight the name using the cursor keys, or mouse.
[ENTER]	Press the Enter key to load the worksheet.

Table 25-1:   Load SHOW worksheet

4.   After loading the worksheet, review it to make sure you know where the input cells are located. The input cells are colored differently than the rest of the cells on a color monitor. The first time you use the worksheet, most of the cells in the spreadsheet will display "NA", or "#NA", but don't worry. As you enter your input values, the NA's in the output cells will be replaced by calculated values.

Unless you have disabled the worksheet protection, only the input cells can be changed. If you accidentally attempt to change a protected (non-input) cell, the program will display an error message. Press the [ESC] key to return to normal operations.

The input sections of the worksheet for this case are boxed for emphasis in the figures below. Remember that the boxes do not show on the worksheet itself.

Worksheet

	A	B	C	D	E	F
1	Name = SHOW					
2						
3						
4	Tyler Pet Foods, Inc. Market Analysis					
5	Expenditure Levels for Show Circuit Frozen Dog Dinner					
6		Level I	Level II			
7	Item	Dollars	Dollars			
8	Television	#N/A	#N/A			
9	Newspapers/Mags.	#N/A	#N/A			
10	Collateral	#N/A	#N/A			
11	Miscellaneous	#N/A	#N/A			
12	Agency Fees	#N/A	#N/A			
13	Total	#N/A	#N/A			
14						
15	Sales Estimates:					
16	Total dog food sales (Billions)	#N/A				
17	Percent of US sale in Boston	#N/A	%			
18	Percent of Boston					
19	area Supermarket sales	#N/A	%			
20						
21	Sales by Category Analysis:					
22		National	Boston	Boston Area		
23		Sales	Area	Supermarket		
24		in	Sales in	Sales in		
25	Sales by Category:	Billions	Millions	Millions		
26	Canned	#N/A	#N/A	#N/A		
27	Dry	#N/A	#N/A	#N/A		
28	Moist	#N/A	#N/A	#N/A		
29	Treats	#N/A	#N/A	#N/A		
30	Total	#N/A	#N/A	#N/A		
31						
32	Contribution Margin Analysis:					
33			Premium Priced		Premium Priced	
34			Canned Food		Moist Food	
35		Input	Case	Tub	Case	Tub
36	Show Circuit:					
37	No. of tubs per case	#N/A				
38	No of Ounces per Tub	#N/A				
39	Price to Consumer		#N/A	#N/A	#N/A	#N/A
40	Retailer Gross Profit Margin:					
41	Percent	#N/A	%			
42	Amount		#N/A	#N/A	#N/A	#N/A
43	Price to Retailer		#N/A	#N/A	#N/A	#N/A
44	Brokerage Commission					
45	Percent	#N/A	%			
46	Amount		#N/A	#N/A	#N/A	#N/A
47	Production, Freight, and Packing Costs:		#N/A	#N/A	#N/A	#N/A
48	Total Costs		#N/A	#N/A	#N/A	#N/A
49	Contribution Margin		#N/A	#N/A	#N/A	#N/A
50						

Worksheet -- Continued

	A	B	C	D	E	F
51						
52	**Break Even Analysis for: Premium-priced canned dog food strategy**					
53			**Expenditure**	**Expenditure**		
54			**Level I**	**Level II**		
55	Expenditure level		#N/A	#N/A		
56	Assumption:					
57	Premium-priced canned dog food with a selling					
58	#VALUE!					
59						
60	Break even point in cases		#N/A	#N/A		
61	Break even point in dollars		#N/A	#N/A		
62	Break even share of Boston					
63	supermarket canned food sales		#N/A	#N/A		
64						
65	**Break Even Analysis for: Premium-priced moist dog food strategy**					
66			**Expenditure**	**Expenditure**		
67			**Level I**	**Level II**		
68	Expenditure level		#N/A	#N/A		
69	Assumption:					
70	Premium-priced moist dog food with a selling					
71	#VALUE!					
72	Break even point in cases		#N/A	#N/A		
73	Break even point in dollars		#N/A	#N/A		
74	Break even share of Boston					
75	supermarket moist food sales		#N/A	#N/A		
76						
77	What-If Analysis Part A:					
78	**Estimated Market Share Based on Case Selling Price:**					
79			Breakeven Market Share Percent Based			
80			on Case Selling Price to Consumer			
81	Enter four selling prices		**Selling**	**Expenditure**	**Expenditure**	
82	to the consumer for the		**Price to**	**Level I**	**Level II**	
83	Canned Dog Food strategy.		**Consumer**	**#N/A**	**#N/A**	
84	Canned	Price 1	#N/A	#N/A	#N/A	
85	Dog	Price 2	#N/A	#N/A	#N/A	
86	Food	Price 3	#N/A	#N/A	#N/A	
87	Strategy	Price 4	#N/A	#N/A	#N/A	
88						
89	What-If Analsysis Part B:					
90	**Estimated Market Share Based on Case Selling Price:**					
91			Breakeven Market Share Percent Based			
92			on Case Selling Price to Consumer			
93	Enter four selling prices		**Selling**	**Expenditure**	**Expenditure**	
94	to the consumer for the		**Price to**	**Level I**	**Level II**	
95	Moist Dog Food strategy.		**Consumer**	**#N/A**	**#N/A**	
96	Moist	Price 1	#N/A	#N/A	#N/A	
97	Dog	Price 2	#N/A	#N/A	#N/A	
98	Food	Price 3	#N/A	#N/A	#N/A	
99	Strategy	Price 4	#N/A	#N/A	#N/A	

5.   Type into the spreadsheet your estimates of the inputs using the information from the input forms you filled out in Step 1. Use the cursor keys ⬅, ➡, ⬇, and ⬆ to move to the desired cell location. Type in the number and press either the ⏎ key or one of the cursor keys. Repeat this procedure until all the necessary input cells are filled.

Viewing the Spreadsheet Schedules and Graph

You can press the cursor keys (⬅, ➡, ⬇, and ⬆), or the Page Up ⬆PG↑ and the Page Down ⬇PG↓ keys to move around the worksheet area. Press the Home key to return to the upper left-hand corner of the spreadsheet.

The worksheet contains a graph. Click on the "Chart" tab to see the graph.

Saving the Spreadsheet

After entering your estimates and examining the results, including the graph, save your spreadsheet by using the following commands.

Keystrokes for Excel or 1-2-3W	Comments
⎋ESC ⎋ESC	If the top of the display screen shows one of the command menus, (see the introduction section of the manual) press the Escape key until the menus disappear. Skip this step if a menu is not displayed.
⎇ALT FS	Access the Command menu, the File menu and the Save option.
⏎ENTER	Press Enter to save under the same name. An Excel file is saved with a "XLS" suffix, and a 1-2-3 for Windows file is saved as a "WK4" file.

Table 25-2:   Save SHOW worksheet

Printing the Worksheet

Place the mouse cursor on top of the "Print Worksheet" button to print it, and click on the "Print Chart" button to print the graph. Make sure you have a printer connected and turned on before attempting to print your results.

Bring the results of your analysis to class when the case is discussed.

Input Form for SHOW - Page 1 of 2

```
                     TYLER PET FOODS, INC.
          INPUT FORM for Show Dircuit Frozen Dog Dinner Market Analysis

Enter Expenditure Levels for Introductory Program
          Item          Level I          Level II
                        Dollars          Dollars

Television           _____      _____

Newspapers/Mags.     _____      _____

Collateral           _____      _____

Miscellaneous        _____      _____

Agency Fees          _____      _____



Enter:
Total dog food sales (Billions)              _____

Percent of US sale in Boston                 _____  %

Percent of Boston area Supermarket sales     _____  %



                                          In
Enter Sales in Millions by Category for:  Millions

        Canned                  _____

        Dry                     _____

        Soft-Dry                _____

        Moist                   _____

        Treats                  _____
```

Input Form for SHOW - Page 2 of 2

	Input:	Premium Priced Canned Food Case	Premium Priced Moist Food Case
Show Circuit:			
No. of tubs per case		_____	
No of Ounces per Tub		_____	
Price to Consumer per case		_____	_____
Retailer Gross Profit Margin Percent		_____ %	
Brokerage Commission Percent		_____ %	
Production, Freight, and Packing Costs per case		_____	_____

What-If Analsysis   Part A: Percent of Market Share Based on
                                          Selling Price to Consumer

---

Enter four selling prices   Selling
to the consumer for the   Price to
Canned Dog Food strategy.   Consumer

Canned	Price 1	_____
Dog	Price 2	_____
Food	Price 3	_____
Strategy	Price 4	_____

What-If Analsysis   Part B: Percent of Market Share Based on
                                          Selling Price to Consumer

---

Enter four selling prices   Selling
to the consumer for the   Price to
Moist Dog Food strategy.   Consumer

Moist	Price 1	_____
Dog	Price 2	_____
Food	Price 3	_____
Strategy	Price 4	_____

Output Form for SHOW - Page 1 of 2

Sales by Category:	in Millions	Boston Area Sales in Millions	Boston Area Supermarket Sales in Millions
Canned	_____	_____	_____
Dry	_____	_____	_____
Soft-Dry	_____	_____	_____
Moist	_____	_____	_____
Treats	_____	_____	_____
Total	_____	_____	_____

	Input:	Premium Priced Canned Food		Premium Priced Moist Food	
		Case	Tub	Case	Tub
Show Circuit: No. of tubs per case	_____				
No of Ounces per Tub	_____				
Price to Consumer		____	____	____	____
Retailer Gross Profit Margin: Percent	_____ %				
Amount		____	____	____	____
Price to Retailer		____	____	____	____
Brokerage Commission Percent	_____ %				
Amount		____	____	____	____
Production, Freight, and Packing Costs		____	____	____	____
Total Costs		____	____	____	____
Contribution Margin		____	____	____	____

Output Form for SHOW - Page 2 of 3

Break Even Analysis for:
Premium-priced canned dog
   food strategy

Expenditure
Level I   Level II

_____

_____   _____

Premium-priced canned dog
   food with a selling price
per case of   _____
Break even point in cases

_____   _____

Break even point in dollars

_____   _____

Break even share of Boston
   supermarket sales

_____   _____

Break Even Analysis for:
Premium-priced moist dog
   food strategy

Expenditure
Level I   Level II

_____

_____   _____

Premium-priced moist dog
food with a selling price
per case of   _____
Break even point in cases

_____   _____

Break even point in dollars

_____   _____

Break even share of Boston
   supermarket sales

_____   _____

Output Form for SHOW - Page 3 of 3

What-If Analysis   Part A: Percent of Market Share Based on
                                       Selling Price to Consumer

Enter four selling prices   Selling   Expenditure
to the consumer for the   Price to   Level I   Level II
Canned Dog Food strategy.   Consumer   _____   _____

		Selling Price to Consumer	Level I	Level II
Canned	Price 1	$_____	_____ %	_____ %
Dog	Price 2	$_____	_____ %	_____ %
Food	Price 3	$_____	_____ %	_____ %
Strategy	Price 4	$_____	_____ %	_____ %

What-If Analysis   Part B: Percent of Market Share Based on
                                       Selling Price to Consumer

Enter four selling prices   Selling   Expenditure
to the consumer for the   Price to   Level I   Level II
Moist Dog Food strategy.   Consumer   _____   _____

		Selling Price to Consumer	Level I	Level II
Moist	Price 1	$_____	_____ %	_____ %
Dog	Price 2	$_____	_____ %	_____ %
Food	Price 3	$_____	_____ %	_____ %
Strategy	Price 4	$_____	_____ %	_____ %

Chapter 26:
Cima Mountaineering

Introduction

Managers for Cima Mountaineering, Inc. must decide on a marketing strategy for expansion in the recreational footwear market. Two possible alternatives for analysis are: (1) enter the weekender segment of the hiking boot market, or (2) extend the existing lines of mountaineering and hiking boots.

The spreadsheet helps you analysis each of these two alternatives and computes the present values of each.

How to Use the Worksheet

1.   Fill out the input form provided for this worksheet after reading the case you are analyzing.

2.   If you have not used any of the worksheets in this manual, please review the section of the manual on how to load Microsoft Excel or Lotus 1-2-3 for Windows, and the worksheets provided on the disk.

3.   Load the worksheet program. After the row and column format appears, load the worksheet using the keystrokes shown in the table below. See the section of the manual on how to load worksheets if you experience difficulties.

Keystrokes for Excel or 1-2-3W	Comments
[ALT] FO	Access the Command menu, the File menu and execute the Retrieve command.
CIMA	Either type in the file name, or highlight the name using the cursor keys, or mouse.
[ENTER]	Press the Enter key to load the worksheet.

Table 26-1:   Load CIMA worksheet

4.   After loading the worksheet, review it to make sure you know where the input cells are located. The input cells are colored differently than the rest of the cells on a color monitor. The first time you use the worksheet, most of the cells in the spreadsheet will display "NA", or "#NA", but don't worry. As you enter your input values, the NA's in the output cells will be replaced by calculated values.

Unless you have disabled the worksheet protection, only the input cells can be changed. If you accidentally attempt to change a protected (non-input) cell, the program will display an error message. Press the [ESC] key to return to normal operations.

The input sections of the worksheet for this case are boxed for emphasis in the figures below. Remember that the boxes do not show on the worksheet itself.

Worksheet

	A	B	C	D	E	F
1	Name = CIMA					
2						
3	INPUTS:					
4	Product	WX 550	WX 450	MX 350	HX 100	HX 50
5	Retail Price	#N/A	#N/A	#N/A	#N/A	#N/A
6	Retail Margin %	#N/A	#N/A	#N/A	#N/A	#N/A
7	Cima Selling Price	#N/A	#N/A	#N/A	#N/A	#N/A
8	Costs as percent of					
9	Cima Selling Price					
10	For First Year:					
11	Sales Commisions	#N/A	#N/A	#N/A	#N/A	#N/A
12	Sales Promotions	#N/A	#N/A	#N/A	#N/A	#N/A
13	Materials	#N/A	#N/A	#N/A	#N/A	#N/A
14	Labor, OHD, Transp.	#N/A	#N/A	#N/A	#N/A	#N/A
15						
16	Annual Price Increases Beginning in 1998-99				#N/A	%
17	Annual Cost Increases Beginning in 1998-99				#N/A	%
18	Annual Discount Rate				#N/A	%
19						

5.   Type into the spreadsheet your estimates of the inputs using the information from the input forms you filled out in Step 1. Use the cursor keys ⬅, ➡, ⬇, and ⬆ to move to the desired cell location. Type in the number and press either the ⏎ENTER key or one of the cursor keys. Repeat this procedure until all the necessary input cells are filled.

Viewing the Spreadsheet Schedules and Graph

You can press the cursor keys (⬅, ➡, ⬇, and ⬆), or the Page Up ⬆PG and the Page Down PG⬇ keys to move around the worksheet area. Press the Home key to return to the upper left-hand corner of the spreadsheet.

The worksheet contains a graph. Click on the "Chart" tab to see the graph.

Saving the Spreadsheet

After entering your estimates and examining the results, including the graph, save your spreadsheet by using the following commands.

Keystrokes for Excel or 1-2-3W	Comments
[ESC] [ESC]	If the top of the display screen shows one of the command menus, (see the introduction section of the manual) press the Escape key until the menus disappear. Skip this step if a menu is not displayed.
[ALT] FS	Access the Command menu, the File menu and the Save option.
[ENTER]	Press Enter to save under the same name. An Excel file is saved with a "XLS" suffix, and a 1-2-3 for Windows file is saved as a "WK4" file.

Table 26-2:   Save CIMA worksheet

Printing the Worksheet

Place the mouse cursor on top of the "Print Worksheet" button to print it, and click on the "Print Chart" button to print the graph. Make sure you have a printer connected and turned on before attempting to print your results.

Bring the results of your analysis to class when the case is discussed.

Input Form for CIMA

Name _____

INPUTS:

Product	WX 550	WX 450	MX 350	HX 100	HX 50
Retail Price	____	____	____	____	____
Retail Margin %	____	____	____	____	____

Costs as percent of Cima Selling Price for First Year:

Sales Commisions	____	____	____	____	____
Sales Promotions	____	____	____	____	____
Materials	____	____	____	____	____
Labor, OHD, Transp.	____	____	____	____	____

Annual Price Increases Beginning in 1998-99 _____

Annual Cost Increases Beginning in 1998-99   _____

Annual Discount Rate   _____%

Output Form for CIMA – Page 1 of 2

Analysis to Enter Weekender Segement of Hicking Boot Market

MX 550

Years	1997 -1998	1998 -1999	1999 -2000	2000 -2001	2001 -2002
Unit Price	_____	_____	_____	_____	_____
Unit Cost	_____	_____	_____	_____	_____
Profit Margin	_____	_____	_____	_____	_____
Sales Forecast in Units	_____	_____	_____	_____	_____
Profit, Before Tax	_____	_____	_____	_____	_____
Present Value	_____	_____	_____	_____	_____
Cumulative Present Value	_____	_____	_____	_____	_____

WX 450

Years	1997 -1998	1998 -1999	1999 -2000	2000 -2001	2001 -2002
Unit Price	_____	_____	_____	_____	_____
Unit Cost	_____	_____	_____	_____	_____
Profit Margin	_____	_____	_____	_____	_____
Sales Forecast in Units	_____	_____	_____	_____	_____
Profit, Before Tax	_____	_____	_____	_____	_____
Present Value	_____	_____	_____	_____	_____
Cumulative Present Value	_____	_____	_____	_____	_____

Summary:

Total Cumulative Present Value	_____	_____	_____	_____	_____

Output Form for CIMA – Page 2 of 2

Name _____

Analysis to Extend Existing Lines of Mountaineering and Hiking Boots

MX 350

Years	1997 -1998	1998 -1999	1999 -2000	2000 -2001	2001 -2002
Unit Price	_____	_____	_____	_____	_____
Unit Cost	_____	_____	_____	_____	_____
Profit Margin	_____	_____	_____	_____	_____
Sales Forecast in Units	_____	_____	_____	_____	_____
Profit, Before Tax	_____	_____	_____	_____	_____
Present Value	_____	_____	_____	_____	_____
Cumulative Present Value	_____	_____	_____	_____	_____

HX 100

Years	1997 -1998	1998 -1999	1999 -2000	2000 -2001	2001 -2002
Unit Price	_____	_____	_____	_____	_____
Unit Cost	_____	_____	_____	_____	_____
Profit Margin	_____	_____	_____	_____	_____
Sales Forecast in Units	_____	_____	_____	_____	_____
Profit, Before Tax	_____	_____	_____	_____	_____
Present Value	_____	_____	_____	_____	_____
Cumulative Present Value	_____	_____	_____	_____	_____

HX 50

Years	1997 -1998	1998 -1999	1999 -2000	2000 -2001	2001 -2002
Unit Price	_____	_____	_____	_____	_____
Unit Cost	_____	_____	_____	_____	_____
Profit Margin	_____	_____	_____	_____	_____
Sales Forecast in Units	_____	_____	_____	_____	_____
Profit, Before Tax Present Value	_____	_____	_____	_____	_____
Cum. Present Value	_____	_____	_____	_____	_____
Total Present Value	_____	_____	_____	_____	_____

Chapter 27:
Colgate-Palmolive Canada: Arctic Power Detergent

Introduction

Brand management for Colgate-Palmolive Canada's Arctic Power detergent is faced with two critical marketing decisions: (1) to continue developing the brand in regional markets or go national, and (2) to use a single or dual positioning strategy for the brand. Arctic Power, a laundry detergent designed for cold water washing, has a strong share in Quebec, the Maritimes, and British Columbia (B.C.), and a marginal share in the rest of Canada.

How to Use the Worksheet

1.   Fill out the input form provided for this worksheet after reading the case you are analyzing.

2.   If you have not used any of the worksheets in this manual, please review the section of the manual on how to load Microsoft Excel or Lotus 1-2-3 for Windows, and the worksheets provided on the disk.

3.   Load the worksheet program. After the row and column format appears, load the worksheet using the keystrokes shown in the table below. See the section of the manual on how to load worksheets if you experience difficulties.

Keystrokes for Excel or 1-2-3W	Comments
[ALT] FO	Access the Command menu, the File menu and execute the Retrieve command.
COLGATE	Either type in the file name, or highlight the name using the cursor keys, or mouse.
[ENTER]	Press the Enter key to load the worksheet.

Table 27-1:   Load COLGATE worksheet

4.   After loading the worksheet, review it to make sure you know where the input cells are located. The input cells are colored differently than the rest of the cells on a color monitor. The first time you use the worksheet, most of the cells in the spreadsheet will display "NA", or "#NA", but don't worry. As you enter your input values, the NA's in the output cells will be replaced by calculated values.

Unless you have disabled the worksheet protection, only the input cells can be changed. If you accidentally attempt to change a protected (non-input) cell, the program will display an error message. Press the [ESC] key to return to normal operations.

The input sections of the worksheet for this case are boxed for emphasis in the figures below. Remember that the boxes do not show on the worksheet itself.

Worksheet

	A	B	C	D	E	F
1	Name = COLGATE					
2						
3	Colgate-Palmolive Canada: Arctic Power Detergent Analysis					
4						
5	Industry Demand Trends:			1986	1987	1988
6	Annual increase in Litres	#N/A	%			
7	Unit Volume in Litres			#N/A	#N/A	#N/A
8	Factory Sales - 1986			#N/A		
9						
10	Arctic Power Estimates:			1986	1987	1988
11	Market Share Percent			#N/A	#N/A	#N/A
12	Litres			#N/A	#N/A	#N/A
13	1986 Factory Sales			#N/A		
14	Factory Price per Litre			#N/A		
15	Projected Factory Sales				#N/A	#N/A
16						
17	Pro forma Income Statement for Arctic Power for 1987 and 1988.					
18		Parameter		1987	1988	1988
19	Sales			#N/A	#N/A	#N/A
20	Cost of Goods sold	#N/A	%	#N/A	#N/A	#N/A
21	Gross Margin			#N/A	#N/A	#N/A
22	Marketing Expenses:					
23	Media expenditures	#N/A	%	#N/A	#N/A	#N/A
24	Trade Promotions	#N/A	%	#N/A	#N/A	#N/A
25	Consumer promotions	#N/A	%	#N/A	#N/A	#N/A
26	Total Marketing Expenses			#N/A	#N/A	#N/A
27	Brand contribution after marketing expenses			#N/A	#N/A	#N/A
28						
29				What-If Analysis: Income as Arctic Power		
30				1988 Market Share Changes		
31						
32					1988 Sales	1988 Income
33					#N/A	#N/A
34				6.50	#N/A	#N/A
35	Changes in 1988 Arctic Power			6.80	#N/A	#N/A
36	Market Share Percent			7.00	#N/A	#N/A
37				7.20	#N/A	#N/A
38				7.40	#N/A	#N/A
39						

5.   Type into the spreadsheet your estimates of the inputs using the information from the input forms you filled out in Step 1. Use the cursor keys ⬅, ➡, ⬇, and ⬆ to move to the desired cell location. Type in the number and press either the ENTER key or one of the cursor keys. Repeat this procedure until all the necessary input cells are filled.

Viewing the Spreadsheet Schedules and Graph

You can press the cursor keys (⬅, ➡, ⬇, and ⬆), or the Page Up ⟦PG↑⟧ and the Page Down ⟦PG↓⟧ keys to move around the worksheet area. Press the Home key to return to the upper left-hand corner of the spreadsheet.

The worksheet contains a graph. Click on the "Chart" tab to see the graph.

Saving the Spreadsheet

After entering your estimates and examining the results, including the graph, save your spreadsheet by using the following commands.

Keystrokes for Excel or 1-2-3W	Comments
⟦ESC⟧ ⟦ESC⟧	If the top of the display screen shows one of the command menus, (see the introduction section of the manual) press the Escape key until the menus disappear. Skip this step if a menu is not displayed.
⟦ALT⟧ FS	Access the Command menu, the File menu and the Save option.
⟦ENTER⟧	Press Enter to save under the same name. An Excel file is saved with a "XLS" suffix, and a 1-2-3 for Windows file is saved as a "WK4" file.

Table 27-2:   Save COLGATE worksheet

Printing the Worksheet

Place the mouse cursor on top of the "Print Worksheet" button to print it, and click on the "Print Chart" button to print the graph. Make sure you have a printer connected and turned on before attempting to print your results.

Bring the results of your analysis to class when the case is discussed.

Input Form for COLGATE

Name _____

Colgate-Palmolive Canada: Arctic Power Detergent Analysis

Industry Demand Trends:
Annual industry increase in Litres   _____ %

Industry unit volume in litres $_____

Industry factory sales - 1986 $_____

Arctic Power estimates of market share as a percent:

        for 1986   _____ %

        for 1987   _____ %

        for 1988   _____ %

        Artic Power 1986 Factory Sales
          in Dollars $_____

Artic Power estimates as Percent for:
    Cost of Goods sold   _____ %

Artic Power estimates of marketing
    Expenses as a percent for:
    Media expenditures   _____ %

   * Trade Promotions   _____ %

    Consumer promotions   _____ %

Output Form for COLGATE

Name _____

Pro forma Income Statement for Arctic Power for 1987 and 1988.

	Parameter	1987	1988	1988
Sales		$_____	$_____	____ %
Cost of Goods sold	____ %	_____	_____	____ %
Gross Margin		$_____	$_____	____ %
Marketing Expenses: Media expenditures	____ %	_____	_____	____ %
Trade Promotions	____ %	_____	_____	____ %
Consumer promotions	____ %	_____	_____	____ %
Total Marketing Expenses		_____	_____	____ %
Brand contribution after marketing	$_____	$_____	____ %	

What-If Analysis: Income as Arctic Power
1988 Market Share Changes

	1988 Sales	1988 Income
1988 sales and income at this percent ____ %	$_____	$_____
1988 sales and income at this percent ____ %	$_____	$_____
1988 sales and income at this percent ____ %	$_____	$_____
1988 sales and income at this percent ____ %	$_____	$_____
1988 sales and income at this percent ____ %	$_____	$_____